Other Books by Geoffrey Bellman

Getting Things Done When You Are Not in Charge
The Beauty of the Beast
Your Signature Path
The Quest for Staff Leadership

THE
CONSULTANT'S
Calling

THE
CONSULTANT'S
Calling

Bringing Who You Are
to What You Do

**New
and
Revised
Edition**

GEOFFREY M.
BELLMAN

Foreword by Peter Block

JOSSEY-BASS
A Wiley Company
www.josseybass.com

Published by

JOSSEY-BASS
A Wiley Company
989 Market Street
San Francisco, CA 94103-1741

www.josseybass.com

Jossey-Bass books and products are available through most bookstores. To contact Jossey-Bass directly, call (888) 378-2537, fax to (800) 605-2665, or visit our website at www.josseybass.com.

Substantial discounts on bulk quantities of Jossey-Bass books are available to corporations, professional associations, and other organizations. For details and discount information, contact the special sales department at Jossey-Bass.

We at Jossey-Bass strive to use the most environmentally sensitive paper stocks available to us. Our publications are printed on acid-free recycled stock whenever possible, and our paper always meets or exceeds minimum GPO and EPA requirements.

Library of Congress Cataloging-in-Publication Data

Bellman, Geoffrey M., 1938-
    The consultant's calling : bringing who you are to what you do /
Geoffrey M. Bellman ; foreword by Peter Block.—New and rev. ed.
       p. cm.—(The Jossey-Bass business & management series)
    Includes bibliographical references and index.
    ISBN 0-7879-5847-6 (alk. paper)
    1. Business consultants. 2. Consultants. I. Title. II. Series.
HD69.C6 B45 2002
  001—dc21   2001004221

SECOND EDITION
PB Printing 10 9 8 7 6 5 4 3 2 1

The Jossey-Bass
Business & Management Series

Contents

Foreword   xiii
   Peter Block
Preface   xix
Introduction: In Pursuit of Purpose   xxvii

Part One
A Foundation for Your Work

1 Creating Your Balanced Life   3
2 Creating the Right Work   13
3 Setting Your Work Boundaries   23
4 Managing Your Calendar   36
5 Making Money   43

The Clients

6 Why Clients Hire You   59
7 Why Clients Keep You   68
8 Building Trust with Clients   74

The Consultant

9 Love at Work   81
10 Fear at Work   88
11 Searching Your Shadows   94
12 The Consultant as Leader   102
13 Building Your Power   106
14 Misusing Your Power   116

Partnership

15 Building Long-Term Partnerships   133
16 Making Rewarding Partnerships   143
17 Avoiding Painful Partnerships   150

Part Five

Understanding Organizations

18 How Organizations Work   159
19 What Works When Creating Change   173
20 How *Not* to Create Change   189

Part Six

The Marketplace

21 You and the Marketplace 195
22 Making The Leap into Consulting 203
23 Stepping Back from Consulting 216

Part Seven

Closing

24 The Quest for Meaning Through Work 227

Sixty Thoughts About Life and Work 229
Resources 233
The Author 237
Index 239

Foreword

In this new edition, Geoff expands and deepens his belief that consulting is more a human endeavor than a technical one. The book serves almost as a memoir to his practice, which offers a model of balance and sincerity that redeems some of the questionable and exploitative aspects of the work.

Consulting is a much maligned profession—and for good reason. For one thing, it is too easy to enter the profession. All it takes is the cost of some stationery and a business card. The term *consultant* is also used to cover a wide range of sins. Out-of-work executives call themselves consultants while they are between jobs, brokers of financial products call themselves consultants to mask their aggressive selling effort, and in general when people take our money and we are not quite sure we got anything of value in return, we call those people "consultants." The fundamental problem facing the consulting profession is that of integrity. This holds whether our consultants operate on their own as external consultants or are internal to a company. In fact, the larger the consulting firm and the larger its reputation, the greater our distrust.

The Consultant's Calling is an answer to the problem of discovering integrity and "value added" in the consulting profession. On its surface, the book lists a hundred and one helpful hints on how to be a successful consultant. But that is not the strength of the book. The book is unique and valuable because it is an unvarnished expression of the integrity and spirituality of its author. The book in its style and form is an example of the consulting/living philosophy that is advocated by its author. What Geoff calls for in his advice on how to consult he embodies in his way of dialogue and confession with the reader. This congruence, ensuring that words and behavior are of one spirit, is just what is too often missing in the consulting profession. The lack of integrity in consulting is of the nature that consultants exploit the client by serving their own economic or self-esteem needs rather than place service to the client as the single-minded purpose of the engagement.

What this should mean for consultants is that the person is the product. Who we are when we are with our clients is the essence of what we are selling. Clients buy when they feel understood. How we respond to clients during the sales call is their best indication of how we will function under pressure in the middle of a project. Clients push on us and test us, and our task is to stand firm, to let them know who we are, what values and viewpoints we represent, and in doing this to let them know that they can lean on us. *The Consultant's Calling* is a long paragraph on what this process looks like and how it feels. The book is homespun and folksy in its style, which lets us know that the person of the author is present. Once again, this has meaning not just because it makes the book easy to digest but because its approach stands as a metaphor for the way consultants need to be with their clients. Homespun and folksy may not be your style—you may be sophisticated and elegant—but each time the unvarnished essence of a person shines through the written word, it creates a voice and song worth hearing.

In addition to the question of integrity, the consulting profession faces the challenge of joining the abstract with the concrete. It is one thing to see a problem clearly; it is another to act on it successfully. In a broader sense, this is the problem with our lives. How do we take the values and beliefs that we have always embraced and express them in the day-to-day, moment-to-moment happenings of our work? This longing is within each of us, and we seek to satisfy it through our work with our clients. The essentially irrational belief is that if I can help my clients live out their own vision, then I will have through that process learned to live out mine.

A good example of this is longing for our freedom. The lure of consulting is that through this way of doing work I will discover my freedom, my personal and work life will be balanced, I will pick and choose the projects I work on, I will have my place by the sea and somehow rediscover my soul. Such a grand illusion. The harsh reality is that most of the consultants we know are the most strung-out people we have met: racing from place to place, worried about the abyss of an empty calendar, trying to act as if each client is their only client, even though they sometimes can't remember the last encounter. The illusion is that freedom can be claimed by changing the structure of our lives. Freedom is more likely to be claimed by acting as if we have a choice, wherever we are, whomever we are with, whatever the task. The act of living out—implementing—our vision and purpose in the given present is how the abstract is made concrete. This is the fundamental message we offer our clients. Too often they don't act on our recommendations because they are waiting for something outside themselves to change. This is an expression of their helplessness. A consultant's primitive offering to the client is to confront this sense of helplessness. The willingness of our clients to choose courage is what makes our recommendations actionable and addresses our longing to be relevant and useful. Geoff offers many paths into the center of this issue.

One other area that is woven into the fabric of *The Consultant's Calling* is embracing the irrational and unconscious aspect of our work. Organizations are a celebration of the engineering mind. They operate on rational models, believe in logic and data as a basis for decisions, and see change as a process of planning, installation, and constant monitoring. It is this exclusive belief in the rational that gets in the way of the very transformations they are seeking. Organizations are human communities, driven as much by intuition and feelings and archetypal urgings as by reason. Our clients need attention at both levels, and consultants, because they operate on the periphery, are in a great position to focus on the more elusive and intangible aspects of a situation. In a way, we are required to be systematic about the irrational parts of work. Geoff takes the stance that consciousness of ourselves is the key to helping clients see clearly the light and dark sides of the challenges they face. This means that clients and consultants are in some ways mirrors of each other. Accepting this, valuing it, and making it explicit is the basis for genuine partnership.

If you have gotten this far through the foreword, you are going to enjoy this book. In its philosophy it affirms the responsibility each of us has for our own lives. This is always hopeful, once we get over the initial shock. Geoff has invited us into the home that is his spirit and shows us that we can make a living being a mainstream radical. I have always thought that the world is changed by those with radical hearts and pin-striped suits, and Geoff is my role model. His book is a triumph of goodwill, wisdom, and a kind of humble Midwestern practicality. If Will Rogers had given attention to the consulting profession, this is the book he would have written.

Mystic, Connecticut   PETER BLOCK
August 2001

To my teachers—
clients,
fellow consultants,
friends,
and family

Preface

How do you thrive as a consultant,
contribute to the world,
make friends, and
become the person you want to be?

Throughout this book, I ask this question of every element of your work. My own consulting career has been a search for the answers to this question. I am bringing the question to you, as well as my best answers to it. The question is *not* "How do you get clients and make money?" As important as those two goals might be, they mean little if they are not in service to contribution, friendship, and integrity. When this book considers the subject of getting clients, it does so with my question in mind. When the book looks at making money, it will be with my question in mind. Your approach to organizations, clients, and change will likely be altered when you see them through the lens of my question.

You can use a career in consulting to enhance your life balance, personal growth, and happiness—if you choose. That is what I have been doing for over twenty years as an independent external consultant. This book builds from my experience, suggesting what you might do to shape a life for yourself with consulting near its center. You are creating a life for yourself right now; this book will help you think about that life, about what you want to create and how to go about doing that.

The Consultant

Most people do not call themselves consultants, but we are *all* busy consulting to each other. Consulting may be as profoundly simple as helping a child learn how to tie a shoe. Or it may be sitting with a friend through tough times. Billions of these small, important consultations occur between people each day. This is not rocket science. At its core, consulting is a natural transaction between people. To be effective, consulting involves at least two individuals— one with a need and an openness to assistance, the other with abilities and a willingness to help. That is what is going on behind all the jargon, technology, projects, view foils, and deadlines so common to consultation in today's organization world.

Consulting must be one of the world's older occupations; people have been giving away help for years. In recent history, thousands of us have begun to collect financial as well as psychic rewards for this help. Some of us regularly receive a paycheck from the one organization we are attempting to help. Others of us ply our wares in a larger marketplace, seeking clients and a living off the fees we collect for the work we do. Whether we are called analysts or auditors, researchers or advisers, programmers or engineers, we are consultants.

Consultants help their clients narrow the gap between what the clients now have and what the clients want or need. Clients choose to be clients; consultants cannot decide for them. Consultants decide which clients they will work with; clients cannot decide for them. Successful consultants choose to work with clients who choose them. This underlying power dynamic affects much of what happens between the two from the moment they start working together.

At one level, becoming an external consultant is as simple as declaring yourself one. There is no widely recognized certification or accreditation required, no respected body to pass judgment, no board review. One of the results is that the marketplace, the Yellow Pages, the Internet, and state employment offices are crammed with consultants. The marketplace decides who will make their living as consultants and who will not. This situation attracts those with a bit of entrepreneurial spirit and unnerves others who do not want to depend on such a fickle employer.

The Calling

The Consultant's Calling is about responding to the voice within, the voice that calls us to pursue meaning and purpose in our lives. This book recognizes the possibility, even the necessity, of achieving much of that meaning through our work. Given that we spend many waking hours working, it makes sense to put those hours in service to a motive higher than money. Given that changes, struggles, and growth are part of the human work experience, why not benefit from that experience in personal as well as profitable ways? Why not recognize our consulting work as a path that leads toward meaning in our lives?

The dictionary tells me that a calling is "a vocation, occupation, trade, or profession." I like that definition because it is wide enough to include most people who work. People can be called to be painters, doctors, farmers, lawyers, preachers, teachers, truck drivers, or consultants. Although the dictionary definition has breadth, it lacks the depth I am trying to convey in the title of this book. I think of my calling as work I love to do, work to which I choose to devote myself. It is work that answers an internal call to "personal greatness," to borrow words from Peter Block. That is how I see my work as a consultant, and that is how I write about it in this book.

You do not have to be called to this consulting work to succeed in doing it. You can approach consulting as the work you do to pay for the life you want to lead. You can commit yourself to consulting as a role you play with organizations, a role you leave behind when you go home to your "real" life. Yes, you can do that, but it seems such a waste when there is so much to gain by allowing your work to be a primary path of contribution and fulfillment.

Some of us have been called but haven't had time to answer. We are so busy doing "it" that we have not paused to figure out what "it" is all about. We put the caller on hold; we will return the call . . . maybe tomorrow. Well, tomorrow is here! This book can help you take the call, to hear that inner voice that calls you to do your work in a way that serves your life. Make the time to figure out what you want, or be forever sentenced to doing what others want. Everyone struggles with the issue of gaining some semblance of control in his or her life. This issue looms especially large for consultants because of their need for clients. You can have what you want and serve your clients too. That is my belief; that is my experience.

Bringing Who You Are to What You Do

Our circumstances have much to do with how we respond in the moment. Circumstances, though influential, are not controlling; we always have a choice, and we always choose. That choice is between an external and internal "me," the me I present to my clients and the me that I keep inside myself. Too often, these two me's do not agree with each other, and I do not act to bring them into agreement. Instead, I put aside the internal me in favor of pleasing others with the external me. This book is about how to change that, how to create more congruence between who you are inside and what you do outside.

I have learned much from other books on consulting, yet I still needed to write a book of my own. I yearned to read more about how consultants lived their lives, found meaning in their work, struggled with their role. As useful as it was to learn about how to start my own business, market myself, contract with clients, and carry out the work, I was looking for something else. I knew that consulting success, narrowly defined and pursued, would not necessarily bring what I wanted. To be successful in this work I needed more than competence and clients and cash flow; I needed to make the work integral to the life I intended to live. I wanted to read about consulting from that viewpoint, so I wrote about it.

Among other things, this book suggests that

You are as powerful as your clients.
You don't need to accept every client who comes your way.

You can pursue your personal growth through your work.
You can build lifelong friendships with clients.
You don't have to work three hundred days a year, or even
     two hundred, or maybe even one hundred to succeed.
Your presence and perspective are as important as your
     skills.

Each of these statements suggests that success is defined within the boundaries of life, not in the marketplace. This is not a pipe dream. Or if it is, I have been successfully fooling myself and others since 1977. That is when I became an external consultant and began learning about, developing, and living by the guidance in this book. Now, almost twenty-five years later, I am reaffirmed in the basic beliefs on which this book builds. When I follow the guidance of my own book, I am richly rewarded. When I put it aside, I pay the consequences.

Readers of This Book

Experienced consultants occasionally need a "tune-up"; they know it is time once again to rethink what they are doing. They know this consulting life suits them, and they want to live it even better. Many of the most appreciative readers of the first edition of *The Consultant's Calling* were those old hands who knew that I knew what I was talking about. They liked the reinforcement this book offered them. Many thanked (or cursed) me for writing the book they had always wanted to write. I believe they will like this second edition, too.

Many readers will be new to this world of external consulting. They have read other useful books about how to set up their business, how to market themselves, and where to find clients with money. This book lets them inside the mind and heart of a more experienced consultant; it reveals what it feels like to do this work. Earlier readers have been reassured by my acknowledgment of my doubts, fears, mistakes, and failures. They liked knowing that they are not alone, that consultants who have been at this for years also struggle. They will be reassured to know that my struggles with consulting have not disappeared in the years since the first edition was published; the struggles have just changed.

The book is also for all of those "undecideds," individuals wondering whether this consulting life might work for them. Because it holds up an unpolished and even homely image of what this work looks like from the inside out, the book will help them imagine what it could be like if they were out on their own.

The book is also written for students, those readers who were assigned it as part of their studies of organizations and change. The first edition became a standard text in graduate courses in business, organization change, and consulting. It was particularly well received by nonresidential master's programs for adults returning to university. My talks with those students have informed this new edition.

Change agent is a bit of consulting jargon often applied to people who are helping change come about in organizations. I count among potential readers those who specialize in systems analysis, information technology, financial analysis, communications, public affairs, engineering, educational technology, health care, labor relations, marketing, public safety, the law, environmental affairs, and public policy. You can see how wide I imagine the audience to be. Many of these specialists will not define themselves as change agents, but they are—and much of this book can help them pursue their specialty even better. Some of my most gratifying responses to the first edition were from technical experts surprised at how well this book dealt with their work and people dilemmas.

Goals for This Book

I want to alter your perspective, to help you see your work in the world a bit differently. I am confident that you will act on any new perspective you gain and value. I am focused not on building your skills but on helping you see where and when to use the skills you already have.

I want to open new meaning in your work and life. I intend to stimulate your thoughts about how your work relates to the rest of your life. I will encourage you to become even clearer than you already are about your underlying values and how they can be acted on through your consulting work. I want you to consider making your work pivotal in your life's purpose, to find work that is truly a calling.

Acknowledgments

I want to bow in the direction of my clients, my friends, my fellow consultants, and my family. They are reliably my best teachers, and I am occasionally their good student. They taught me what I know about doing this work, leading this life. I want to thank my wife and editor, Sheila Kelly; I appear to be a better writer than I am because of her. I am grateful to Susan Williams and Bernadette Walter at Jossey-Bass for their guidance.

Seattle, Washington   GEOFF BELLMAN
August 2001

Introduction:
In Pursuit of Purpose

We are on this earth for a purpose; our life task is to discover what it is. As unique as our individual pursuit might be, we are each just one of billions of people simultaneously searching for purpose . . . and that is what turns the world. And that's where consulting comes in. In large and small ways, consultants help people discover their purpose—at least that is what I think we do.

My own purpose has been to advise people working in organizations. This is not just my job, not just my profession, but my purpose, my calling. I was drawn to this work as strongly as if a magnet were embedded in my body, attracting me to organization forms and functions. The source of my motivation is as mysterious and compelling as that. Why has my fascination continued for so many years? Why do I find myself attracted again and again to work with these huge, maddening, miraculous creatures called organizations? Yesterday I found myself stuck to the side yet another one! It must be the magnet.

When I envision my life, I see myself working; I cannot imagine doing nothing—at least not for long. Consulting has meant self-employment and self-discovery; it has fed my family and my soul. I expect to continue working the rest of my life. For thirty years, I found most of my fulfillment with corporate clients who paid me money; for the last five years almost all my work has been with community clients who pay me compliments. It's all work.

Work, though essential to life, is not life. As important as work is to finding our individual meaning, it twists us out of shape if we let it. This book sees work through a life perspective. I wrote it to help us honor life purposes in our every consulting move. Honoring our life purposes will result in different actions than we would take if we were to honor authority, money, power, tradition, or even friendship. It opens us to alternatives that are unthinkable when consulting is played primarily as a competitive sport. So there it is. I have given away the secret. You have yet to finish the Introduction, and you already know what the rest of the book is about.

You are about to be marinated with and basted in my perspective on consulting. That perspective will seep into your own as you read. I hope you like the flavor and sop it up! When you find that you really like the taste, pause to note why: How does it fit with your preferences and possibilities? And when it gets a little too sweet or sour, remind yourself that this is just one consultant talking; there are many other flavors available. Pay particular attention when you find an idea distasteful—especially if you have an emotional reaction to it like anger or disgust. Although your reactions may simply be revealing where I am off base, they could be clues to areas that you might want to explore more deeply. My own experience shows that when something or someone is distasteful to me, that thing or person often stands for a part of myself with which I have yet to come to terms.

I write to you as to a friend who cares about me and my work, a friend who will accept both my bragging and my complaining. This book is a lopsided conversation in which I imagine your partnership. Granted, you are doing most of the "listening," but I hope you will end up talking with yourself, reflecting on what you learn. You will hear about both my success and my failure in the work. Sometimes we will soar to lofty heights, dreaming about the profound cosmic changes that can be created in organizations. At other times, we will burrow into the minutiae of consulting, wondering what to wear today.

THE
CONSULTANT'S
Calling

Part One

A Foundation for Your Work

One

Creating Your Balanced Life

A s consultants, we have critical choices to make about when, where, and how much to work. Most people with "real jobs" do not have the opportunity and burden that come with these choices. This chapter focuses on small choices and actions that tip the balance of work and life. Our daily work choices affect our life balance profoundly; those little choices express what we value. In life's day-to-day details and decisions, we attempt to realize our values and purpose. Many of the details in my life are about my work: how much of it I do, where and how I do it. In this chapter, you will read about what I have done to manage my consulting time to achieve some life balance. I tell you what has worked for me and what hasn't, so that you can put your experience next to mine.

I paid close attention to the boundaries of my practice; I chose to limit my work in ways quite uncommon among consultants. If you want to hear stories about how to earn big dollars as a consultant, then buy a consulting book that holds out that promise. But if you want to learn about how one consultant finds happiness, growth, and value by working less than most, then read on. Use my practice to gauge your own. What I offer is not "right," but it could be useful in stimulating thoughts about your practice. I tell you about what I have done and help you think about your life/work balance. We begin with the ideas that underpin the actions I describe later in the chapter.

Over my twenty most active years as an external consultant, I chose to work an average of seventy-three paid days a year. What do I call "paid work"? Anything I do for a client. If I am working for a client at my office, at the client's office, or in between, the client expects to be billed for my work. Here is how my twenty years split out.

- Begin with the paid days:
  Years one to three: 100 days
  Year four: 200 days
  Years five to nine: 100 days
  Years ten to sixteen: 60 to 80 days
  Years seventeen to twenty: 40 to 60 days
- Then add the annual unpaid days:
  Marketing, logistics, and administrative time: 30 to 40 days
  Community and professional organizations: 40 to 60 days
- Average total: 150 to 160 days per year

Once when I told someone about my workload, she commented, "Oh, I'm sorry to hear that." She thought that was all the work I could get; she couldn't believe I was turning away work. Sometimes I wonder about my approach too. I could accept twice as much work and make twice as much money. Some friends work about three times as much as I do. Another worked close to three hundred days one year. He remarked, "You are leading a balanced life, and I am getting rich! We are both doing what we choose, and we are both happy! Isn't that great?!" Yes, it is. His money occasionally provokes my envy, and my lifestyle makes him green once in a while. But he is right: we are both happy.

What Are You Choosing?

Think about what you are choosing to do. Don't get trapped in doing the work, just doing it, doing it, doing it. Figure it out! Align your calendar with your purpose. I always return to the basic question of this book: *How do you thrive as a consultant, contribute to the world, make friends, and become the person you want to be?* For me, answering that question has meant working less than the norm, having tea with my wife more often than the norm, parenting children, giving time to the community, writing books, paying off our house and car, saving money, cultivating friendships, and enjoying where I live. Working less has helped me do this. You may want to work 250 days a year. Fine—if you develop in the process, build your relationships with others, and contribute to the world. But if you know your focus on work is hurting you or the people and world around you, then perhaps it is time to rethink what you are doing with your life.

So, you ask, what do I do with the time I am not investing in clients? Here is a very impressive list of activities:

Learn the violin	Climb Mount Rainier	Study leadership Save the salmon
Swim one hundred laps	Talk with the governor	Create a foundation
Meditate	Run ten miles	

But that is not *my* list. Here is my list:

Have tea	Read a book	Answer e-mail
Go out to dinner	Talk with friends	Attend a conference
Fix dinner	Visit my father	Write a book
Make travel plans	Take a nap	Pay bills
Work in the community	Go to a movie	Play with grandchildren
Go for a walk	Fix my computer	Rent a video
	Consider exercising	Worry
	Coach individuals	

This list suits me well. There are a few items on it that you might count as work, such as conferences or writing books. Yes, these activities are good for business, but for me they have never been a source of significant business. Even when I was more fully engaged in the marketplace, I could have stopped all of them and still realized my business goals.

I love this work! I care so much about this work that at this point in my life I do it without being paid for it. This work is a calling. No, I do not need to do it every day; it is not the center of my life. Work is *a* center in my life—and there are other centers. Overall, this approach works for me, but it does have its drawbacks.

The Downsides of Working Less

While other consultants are flying around the country worrying about whether they are spending enough time with their families, or wearing themselves out working too hard, I am worrying too. I seldom see consultants who intentionally restrict their work as much as I do. This causes me to "what if": What if I am being stupid? What if I am not putting enough aside for my later years? What if the family has needs I have not planned for? What if I am playing the grasshopper to everyone else's ant? I have a pattern of worrying about this—it's one of the things I do in my spare time. I get a little anxious when I think about the money I could make working a hundred more days a year. The anxiety is tied to what I think I "should" be doing. That anxiety holds now, even after twenty-five years. I await that call from my financial adviser saying, "I was wrong! You don't have any money! Go out and earn more!"

For those of you inclined to envy my work and lifestyle, know that there are costs beyond the worry I have cited here. First of all, the financial costs: working only a third of the time that others work who have related experience, reputation, and fees means that I make one-third the money. I am well paid for what I do, but so are those other people! And they get three times as much as I do each year! And I notice—and sometimes covet their wealth. I have options regarding what to do with my time; they have options regarding what to do with their money. Whereas they are providing a great margin of safety for themselves, by comparison I live closer to the edge. They readily purchase vacations homes, cars, toys, and travel for themselves and their families. I watch our consumption; I need to live within the tighter limits that come with working seventy-three paid days a year. My peers working two hundred-plus days are less likely to have to do that. My path does require a degree of financial constraint and discipline. Even with these limitations, though, I live quite well.

Working an average of seventy-three days a year has affected the kind of business I do. I am less likely to accept or be engaged in working in-depth on a change project for an organization. If a major change project is like a large lake, you will more likely find me somewhere along the shore or skimming across the tops of the waves rather than plumbing the lake's depths. Seventy-three days spread among a few clients doesn't allow the in-depth engagement that a large change effort requires. As a result, I find my work more centered on events; I often have to give up the in-depth immersion in projects, even though I find that level of work exciting.

The way I work affects how my clients see me. Because they know me only by what I do with them, they know me more narrowly than my actual skills would allow. I am capable of diving in! I want them to know that. But if they asked me to dive deep, would I? Chances are, I would not. You've probably noticed: I want it both ways! My constant dilemma is that I want it both ways and won't let go of either as I make each new decision on each project. I hear my peers talk about their exciting work. Because they have chosen to work three times as much as I do, they have three times as much to talk about, both in quantity and quality. They are diving in! I often feel like the skinny guy on the beach getting sand kicked in his face. And I worry about what those clients to whom I want to be attractive think of me. I have chosen not to dive in, not to take the Charles Atlas Consultant Muscle-Building Workshop. I'll stop before I run this metaphor into the ground, but you get the idea. I am sensitive to the opinions of my peers and clients, and I wonder whether they think I do "real work" or just dabble.

My approach to work takes its toll on my mental discipline. Because I work less than most, my day-to-day work skills are not as finely honed. My life skills are great, but my work skills are used less, and they get flabby. Sometimes I feel less than fit when I am consulting. My investment in my life outside of work can result in a less focused approach to what I do. I was recently working with a consultant from a large, hard-driving consulting firm. I noticed the differences in our approaches. There were advantages to each, but I was aware of the downside of my more social and relaxed approach. Yes, there is an upside too, but that is not my point here.

A last downside is my reduced visibility. I am around less, so my clients think of me less. Being around more often usually results in more work. When I was pulling back to forty days a year, I worried about whether clients would call me at all. They did, but it is still a worry, given the competitiveness of the consulting market. How much work must I do so that clients still see me as a potential contributor? When do they quit thinking about me or forget I am around?

Even with all the concerns I've listed here, I chose to work less. I never wanted to quit. I worked toward being in a position to take work based on my interest and potential contribution. I never tired of the work; I did tire of working for money. Now that I can afford it, I can take on more consulting in nonprofit organizations.

How Much Should You Work?

How do you decide whether to work 40 or 240 days a year? Ask questions: What do you want to do? How much do you need to work? And how much do you want to work? If you want to work less than you are now working, are you willing to give up what those extra days now give you? Do the benefits outweigh the costs?

If you are a one-person consulting firm, there are projects that you do not have the resources to take on. If you plan to work 80 rather than 240 days a year, your availability also limits what you might commit to. For example, a client and I were looking down the road to where our project was headed. Both of us could see that in about six months, a large training effort would be required. I told her that I wanted to help design that part of the project but that I didn't want to do the training. I was uncomfortable giving that much time to one client; the project would have taken most of my work year. Together we agreed to figure out how to get the training resources she would need.

My client could have said, "I want a consulting firm that has the resources I need when I need them! This project requires the concentrated efforts of two or three consultants for three months, not the occasional input of a part-time consultant!" That is a reasonable alternative; I am fortunate that she did not see it that way. The conversation tested my work boundaries; I was uncomfortable holding to them, but glad I did.

My main concern is the impact of my work parameters on the project. Are the alternatives I offer to the client based primarily on what the project needs, or do I limit my offered alternatives to those that I can provide? These questions occur naturally if you are a one-person firm or part of a small firm. They occur more often if you are in a small firm and limit the work you do. I temper my concern about this with the fact that large firms with large resources are faced with their own questions: Are the alternatives we offer based on what the project needs? Do we expand alternatives to create opportunities to use all the resources we have on staff? At that end of the continuum, they must trouble themselves with whether their clients need all the help they provide.

If you are now working forty days a year and want to work over one hundred, you are in a great position to prepare yourself. Present circumstances force you to constrain your spending, to think carefully about how you use your resources. The discipline you develop during these tight times will serve you well later when you are working more. If you are working closer to two hundred days a year and paying your bills, meeting your goals, and feeling happy, then enjoy it.

Put Your Personal Time on Your Calendar First

Regardless of how much you work, make time for yourself your top priority. Not close to the top, but top. If you do not, you will give up your personal time when it is challenged by work. Decide how much time you want for yourself and put it on your calendar now. Whether it is a family vacation, two days a month all to yourself, or an hour each morning, get it on your calendar! Give it the same dignity as all those other (less important) meetings and activities you regularly note there. And do not let go of it when a client calls. Once in a while, you may move personal time to accommodate work, but do not eliminate that time.

Imagine that you have a week of personal time on your calendar, and a client calls with work to do. She wants two days of your time right in the middle of your personal week. Tell her that you are busy that entire week; don't tell her you have a vacation planned. You are busy. From her perspective, you are probably with another client. Offer other dates. Most of the time, the client will select from your available dates. Four out of five times my clients go with this option, and I do not have to give up the week I planned. But let's imagine that your clients hold on to the date they proposed. Tell them you will check on moving your other engagement and call them back. You do not have to decide on the phone. Hang up, go to your calendar, search for another time to take your personal week, talk to others involved, set up the new personal time, and call your client back and say the week is now available. Be sure to move the week to another spot on your calendar. If you simply erase it without placing it in another week, you are declaring by your action that your personal time needn't be on your calendar, needn't be respected. If you show a pattern of regularly moving your personal time around in favor of work, you are indicating that work time is more important than personal time—regardless of what you may be telling yourself or your friends and family. So get your personal time on your calendar and honor it; doing so can make a great difference in your life balance.

Creating the
Right Work

onsulting work is about succeeding as yourself, being yourself more often than playing a role. We all play roles; they are useful in real life as well as theater. The challenge is not only to play roles of others' creation but also to create roles that fit with who we are. I frequently play the role of "consultant," a role widely recognized in the organization world. I know what that role is, and so do many clients and potential clients. Good work comes my way partly because the clients and I agree on the role of the consultant in their organization. The role of consultant—how one speaks, listens, dresses, and acts—can be defined entirely on the client's terms. That's one way of doing it, but where is "succeeding as yourself" in that process?

An early task, with ourselves and later with clients, is to define the role so that we can live within it. When you can be yourself and be a consultant at the same time, you do not have to pretend. Choosing to put on a consulting role that does not fit is like wearing a suit of armor. It may be the legitimate costume for fighting the dragons at hand, but if it does not fit you, you will end up more exhausted than successful. That's what happens when you and I choose not to be ourselves but choose instead to play a heavy consultant role that does not fit. In less medieval times and terms, the costume may be a pressed suit, a confident stride, and a painted smile. If inside you do not match the pressed, confident, and painted exterior, the role will be a burden. It may be a burden you are willing to take on, but still a burden. Carry this role day after day, month after month, and its weight increases.

Establish a consulting role that asks you to be—to "play"—yourself. Being a consultant is more comfortable than playing one. Even if you play the consultant role very well, if it is not you, it is still an act. When the costume and the script regularly differ dramatically from what you are thinking and feeling, you will suffer the consequences. We all do this, but being more conscious of what we are choosing to do makes it less likely that we will carry too many role burdens. Consulting can provide us the opportunity to be ourselves, but we have to make that opportunity.

Role playing, in the pretending way I have been describing it, is focused on meeting others' needs while hiding my own. When I do this over the course of a long project, I pretend that my needs are being met. When I do this in my life, my life loses its unique meaning because I am not giving expression to myself.

Learning a new role, or a new aspect of your role, can expand who you are; it can be worth the added work. For example, when working on a project that involved virtual teams, I had to supplement what I knew about intact, face-to-face teams with the new options and consequences that come with people working at a distance and online. Doing this work stretched my role beyond its former definitions. I learned in the process; my thoughts were expanded in the process. This took extra effort and was worth it. If I had played the role of the consultant who knows everything about virtual teams, my burden would have been much heavier. Instead, I defined my role in a way that included learning along with my experience. My authenticity came through, and I avoided pretense.

Self-Assessment

We consultants need to understand who we are and what we bring to others. We are not unique in this respect, but it is important to us if we are to survive in the marketplace. We need to be able to think about our abilities and talk about them with our clients, so that we can decide what work to pursue. We need to keep track of how we are reaching for our life goals through our work. This means staying in touch with the primary tool of our trade: ourselves.

When I can step back far enough to gain perspective on myself, I notice that my self-assessment is fairly consistent through time. I regularly give myself blame or praise for the same vices and virtues. My earlier life training makes it easy for me to find fault with myself; I can build the debit list quickly, though I am reluctant to write it down. That same past training tends to block expression of my positive characteristics. My strengths are what will sustain me through difficult times, however, so I need to acknowledge them. My strengths are what will allow me to succeed in the work I do, not all those weaknesses that I hope to eventually repair.

We should be able to look our strengths as well as our weaknesses in the eye. When others are interested, we should be able to articulate who we are and what we do well, and own up to who we are not and what we do not do well. Thinking about when and how to bring our talents to the workplace should provoke more excitement than anxiety. A confident self-assessment helps on all these levels.

A part of how we see ourselves is how we think others see us. A match between my self-assessment and how others actually see me is useful. We often erroneously assume there is a match between how we see ourselves and how others see us. Check it out. Find out how others see you and how they think you see yourself. Consider the same points yourself: How do you see yourself, and how do you think you are seen? You are always telling clients how you see them, so turning that around seems reasonable. If you are not getting the candid information you need, keep asking.

Our livelihoods depend on accurate readings of our clients' perceptions of us. We need to know how we are coming across. It could be that our impact on the client is negative. If we know this, we can work with it. If we do not know it, we will work with the inaccurate readings we have taken. But all of this about client perception must be built on the foundation of a solid self-assessment. What follows is a self-assessment that finds out more about who you are and identifies work you would like to do in the future.

Finding the Right Work: An Exploration

If thinking more deeply about your uniqueness and your work as a consultant sounds appealing, I offer you ten steps for doing so. Use them entirely or separately. Set aside time to complete each step, time that is outside the regular rush of your day. This exploration will pay off only if you bring time and attention to it. Let's begin with a declaration:

1. *You are unique.* Don't worry about *whether* you are unique; we will consider *how.* Put aside the anxiety that comes with wondering, "What could be special about me?" I am familiar with that worry, and it has gotten me nowhere! Assume you are unique and that exploring your uniqueness is worth doing.

2. *Ask yourself, How am I unique?* This question is asking about you, the person—not you, the consultant or potential consultant. That comes later. Your consulting uniqueness will flow out of your personal uniqueness. In answering this question, list qualities, traits, ambitions, styles, goals, characteristics—anything you think might define what is uniquely you. Build a description that could not be about anyone else. Spend some reflective time working on this question. If you don't, this step will not work.

3. *Ask others, "What is unique about me?"* Ask relatives and friends this question in whatever way suits you and them, but do ask it. Notice your feelings of comfort or discomfort with doing so. If you feel uncomfortable, remind yourself that clients are asking this question about consultants all the time; the answers they come up with include the reasons you will be hired—and not hired. Here is your opportunity to receive some answers aloud from people you care about and trust. Talk with at least five of them and take notes.

4. *Look at what you have learned.* Look for patterns in what you have heard from others. How do their comments fit with each other? And with your comments on yourself? What do you particularly like and dislike in what you have heard? Take all the notes you have thus far—from yourself

and others—and rewrite them in some integrated, organized way. This might be a list or three paragraphs or a drawing or a diagram; it's up to you. Whatever you put down should express who you are in a way that distinguishes you from other people. Get it down on one page.

5. *Get confirmation.* Ask someone you talked to in step three to look at and comment on your page. Does it capture your uniqueness from his or her perspective? Then test your page with two more people and notice their reactions. If your page doesn't fit with their reactions, go back over earlier steps; think more about yourself, talk with people again, rewrite your page. Remember that in the end the page needs to fit you; you need to feel the fit. If what you have prepared fits for you and others, put it aside and move on to the next steps.

6. *Ask yourself, What consulting work do I want to do?* This is your "wish list." Put aside your considerations from earlier steps and ask yourself what consulting work you want to do. Forget whether you are presently prepared to do that work. What do you *want* to do? Writing about it will help you become clearer. You may find this question helpful: What would a consulting week look like in five years if you were doing the work you really want to do? Write it down as a list.

7. *From the consulting work you want, what are you ready to do now?* This is your "ready list." Highlight each item on your wish list that falls within your current interests and capabilities. Notice how many wish list items are highlighted. Many of us find that our ready list is considerably shorter than our wish list. So be it! This is the kind of clarity we need so as to take useful action.

8. *From the consulting work available, what are you willing to do?* This is your "willing list." Consider the marketplace and the work available out there. If you don't

know much about it, find out from other consultants. Consider the many kinds of work available and note any work that you are capable of doing but do not really want to do—in other words, work that could be added to your ready list but that would not make your wish list. For example, you do not want to do subcontracting work for others, but you are ready and willing to do it in the short term while building your skills and practice toward fulfilling your wish list.

9. *Match uniqueness and readiness.* Put your descriptive page from step four beside your ready list from step seven: How well does the work you want to do and are able to do right now connect with your uniqueness? Mark the strong connections; these are your opportunities to become yourself while consulting. These connections are essential to your motivation. Strong connections suggest the consulting work you ought to pursue. Few strong connections suggest that you reconsider what you do in the near term, perhaps focusing on the learning discussed in the tenth step. Your "willing list" from step eight may help as well.

10. *What do you need to learn?* Put your descriptive page from step four beside your wish list for step six: What are the developmental opportunities for you to plan on over the next few years? Note the gaps that particularly intrigue you. Which would you like to work on soon? Which ones require longer-term plans and resources? If you have many gaps to close, it is important that you begin soon. Identify a few areas where you can begin and learn fast; this will increase your motivation to do even more. Ask more experienced people to help you with this step.

The thinking and planning and action involved in these ten steps prepare us to face the marketplace. Too often we jump into the marketplace in a reactive mode. Preparing before we step out into the world helps us develop options, seek what we want, and avoid being tossed about. The marketplace offers a wealth of opportunity but does not care about us. We have to care for ourselves, to prepare ourselves if we are to succeed.

Your Strengths Are Also a Vulnerability

When I consider where I might most need to grow, I am inclined to start listing my weaknesses, with the idea that working on a few of them would make me a better consultant or a better husband or a more complete person. The gaps between what I am doing and what I would like to be doing are apparent and uncomfortable. I usually have a handful of these acknowledged gaps that I promise myself I will work on.

I also have areas in which I see myself as strong. My life experience, aided by others' feedback, helps me build images of my strength. I celebrate many of these strengths just as I castigate myself for my weaknesses. And I move in my world with confidence in these strengths. Personal growth opportunities often show up where I do not expect to find them; they come from my strengths! My alleged strengths traitorously creep up from behind and stab me where I am most vulnerable. My major growth "opportunities" are often in areas where I think I am doing very well. It's often those parts of my world that I believed I have stitched together most tightly that start coming apart. Why?

My confidence in my strengths dulls my attention to their expression and their consequences. When I "know" I have a particular skill, I am inclined to put it on automatic pilot and concentrate my full attention elsewhere. Sometimes confidence in one's ability becomes overconfidence and produces unintended results: the consultant who relates so well to his clients that they both lose track of what they are trying to accomplish; the extremely insightful manager who succeeds in turning off his entire team by being extremely insightful; the consultant so enamored with her model that she does not hear the client's concerns; the articulate and clever person who dominates conversations with words and wit, leaving no room for others' contributions.

In each of these cases, a real strength led to unintended consequences. Each of these people was shocked to find that what he or she did so well was what in fact produced the unintended results. They overused their strengths. The growth opportunity that comes from these quarters is disorienting and unexpected. To find that a strength has become a liability can upset our personal confidence, disrupt our internal order, and put our egos in a tailspin.

This message does not apply exclusively to consultants, but its application to us is particularly clear. Clients hire us to use our professional abilities; sometimes these finely honed abilities hinder as well as help us. Excessive pride in or passion for our work creates distance between us and our clients, preventing us from achieving the results we want so much to deliver.

Improve your performance by recognizing and refining your strengths, rather than by just repairing your weaknesses. In fact, look first to strengths when considering self-development. When you have a skill that you and others acknowledge, give that skill special attention: learn more about it, when and how to use it best, and how not to abuse it. Your positive uniqueness has to do with abilities you currently possess rather than those you have not yet learned. Learn what makes you special, why others value you, why you value yourself, and build on this authentic foundation. The motivation and energy naturally flowing from these sources leads to your being hired to do what you know how to do and want to do. Assess yourself and build your business around your abilities and aspirations. Do not begin by looking in the marketplace to be told what you ought to be; start by looking at yourself and what you want to be, then go to the marketplace. The marketplace will tell you what it wants, but it will not operate in your best interests; only you can do that.

Three

Setting Your Work Boundaries

*W*hen you cross a boundary, a change takes place. You were "in"; now you are "out." On this side it's "yes," and on that side it's "no." This chapter helps you define the boundaries of your work by considering such questions as, What work do you want and not want? What work will you accept and not accept? Where do you want to work? How much do you want to work? What kind of clients do you want and not want?

The notion of work boundaries seems foreign to many consultants. They have told me that they seldom, if ever, say no to work. Some were bragging, some were complaining, and they all were quite sure what they would do the next time the phone rang with a potential client on the other end of the line: they would say yes to the work. Why? "I want to be helpful." "I can't afford not to." "When people have problems, I can't turn them away." "I am flattered that they asked me." "I don't want to reject them." "I want them to call me again." "I don't want them to reject me." "If I say no today, will there be other work tomorrow?" "I like doing this work so much." "They need me." "I simply cannot form the word *no* with my lips." All these reasons come from successful consultants.

And here's what else I hear—often from those same consultants: "I am overworked." "This year has been so stressful!" "My life is out of control." "I need a vacation but can't schedule it for three months." "My family is upset." "I need more personal time." "My love life? Hah!" "The travel is killing me!" "I'm not sleeping." When you consider these comments in relation to those in the preceding paragraph, what possibilities come to mind? Saying no more often might be a useful way for yes-prone consultants to bring more of what they want into their lives. If you cannot say no, can you really say yes? If you accept every piece of work that comes your way, are you really choosing? It appears to be a choice, but when you always say yes, is no really a possibility? Are you truly choosing, or are you compelled? I suspect that neither you nor your clients want a consultant who can say nothing but yes.

It is not easy for me to say no either. Too often I say yes when I should have said no, and find myself caught in a project that I would rather not be doing. When I think about it, the clues were usually there at the beginning; I knew why I shouldn't do the work, but I said yes anyway. Over the years, some patterns have emerged that, if I pay attention to them, can help me say no early and avoid doing work I really do not want to do. Perhaps reading about some of my boundaries will help you with your own. Think about the work patterns you are forming and the boundaries they suggest. You increase your clarity and power as a consultant when you draw the lines around your practice—lines that can bend and move, but lines nevertheless.

Time Boundary

Time is one of the most tangible and measurable of the boundaries; you can count the hours and days if you wish. Regardless of what you are doing during those hours (the subject of other boundaries), the sheer quantity of hours is shaping your practice and your bottom line. To put it simply, how much do you want to work? How much are you willing to work? How much must you work? Will you work weekends? Holidays? Evenings? The next chapter of this book elaborates on how you might better control your time.

Fee Boundary

This second boundary is also quantifiable and important enough to warrant an upcoming chapter. What do you want to be paid? What are you willing to be paid? How much must you be paid? Do your fees vary by client? By type of work? Because your gross income is determined by your fees multiplied by the time you work, this is a bottom-line boundary. The time and fee boundaries have much to do with your overall quality of life.

Work Boundary

Now we are moving into discussion of boundaries that are a little harder for us to see and understand together. We all work hours and get paid in dollars, but we do many different types of work. You will work better with clients if you know before meeting them which types of work you want to do, are willing to do, and do not want to do. By "type of work" I mean the content of the work, the depth of engagement with the client, the process you use in doing the work. This is an important boundary to draw because it is always changing, not only in the marketplace but also within you. What you want to do this year, you may tire of next year. This year everybody wants your favorite work; next year nobody does. Perhaps family considerations dictate a certain type of work for the next five years—work you were not interested in earlier.

For example, when I find myself regretting having taken on work, it is often a small to medium-size project—one to five days of work. This has happened often enough that I now look at those opportunities differently. In contrast, I seldom regret my commitment to major projects. This is probably because I tend to check out large projects more carefully and to accept small ones too readily—partly because they are small. Often that small piece of work ends up taking more time than I expected or contracted for—more time than it should take. Sometimes I do not or cannot charge clients for the extra time because the cost would exceed our contract or would be exorbitant from their perspective. So in the interests of great outcomes, I do part of the work for nothing—adding to my exasperation. Even payment for this time is little solace, because all through the project I know I should not have chosen it. Consider what patterns you have: When do you accept work that gets in the way of the practice you are trying to develop?

Another example: if I had accepted all the work that came my way in early years, today I would be a management trainer rather than an organizational consultant. People call consultants because they have a need they hope consultants can help with. Almost all of my early calls were to do training. Following that lead would have made me a trainer. I redirected my practice only by saying no to training and yes to consulting. Standing back from the business and reflecting on what I wanted gave me the strength to say no to many lucrative training opportunities. Consider what you want to do and compare that to your patterns of work acceptance: Are you defining your work boundary clearly enough to shape your business as you want it? The focus here is on asking yourself what type of work you *want* to do as opposed to what you are willing to do or do not want to do.

Client Boundary

If you pay close attention, you will see patterns emerge in the types of clients with whom you work well—and not so well. Some of us work better in the not-for-profit world, others with government, others with the for-profit sector. Or you may do particularly well with engineers or educators or social workers. Let your experiences be your guide. For example, I have difficulty in the health care industry, especially at the middle to lower levels of their organizations. Although the results working there have ranged from satisfactory to terrific, my feelings during the work are laced with discomfort. I have concluded that I should leave health care to someone more attracted to it and comfortable in it. I usually turn down work in health care for this reason and recommend someone better suited.

Another pattern of mine: I do not work that well with hourly workers. I like working with them, and I'm not very good at it. So this is not a matter of preference but one of effectiveness. My patterns here suggest I'd be better off focusing on management and leaving the hourly people to someone else. Consider: To which clients are you more and less attracted? With whom do you work well—and not so well—in organizations? With what types of clients do you want to work? With what types of clients are you willing to work, or unwilling to work?

Reflect on your experience, and I predict you'll see patterns that will help you make better decisions in the future. If you are new to this work, the patterns may not be well formed or evident. Even after years of consulting experience, you will find you still have to stop and analyze your data to learn and shape the boundaries of your practice.

Work Location Boundary

Deciding the physical locations of your work determines another boundary of your practice. Boundaries are geographic even in this Internet age. As you pursue your work, you face these questions: How far will you travel to do your work: To your computer? To your home office? To your office across town? Would you travel to a client an hour away? How about a client across the country? Or across the world? You know some of those answers now—both what they are and what you would like them to be—and you use those answers to determine whether a potential client operates within your boundaries.

Travel—whether it is taking a connecting flight across the country or driving across town—is grueling and getting more so. Choosing to travel does not make traveling easy, but at least you recognize that this is the option you chose. Travel affects your life and your energy. Two hours in evening traffic can take the remaining energy that would have been available to family or friends. One day of work across the country can take two full days with travel, not to mention leaving home early or arriving late—and changing time zones. Think about why you would, and would not, want to travel as you read about some of the choices I have made.

I have chosen to travel to my work—primarily west of the Mississippi River—for many reasons. The client base where I live is not large enough to support me in the diversity of work I want to pursue. I see a greater risk of being pigeonholed by local clients, of having my reputation built on this narrow base—and of being seen as narrower. Other markets support higher fees than the local market. There is the recognition that comes with being the expert from out of town; I like it, and my clients do too. My local clients like knowing that people across the country hire me; travel defines me as a national consultant. Most of all, I like being able to dedicate myself to my clients while I am in their city. I do not have to worry about getting home to fix dinner, and I usually don't have to face rush-hour traffic. Quiet evenings alone in my room with room service are appealing too.

But there is another side to this. A year after moving to Seattle, I was tied up in the traffic in Houston, creeping toward the airport along with (apparently) everyone in town. A light dawned: "I didn't move to Seattle to spend all this time in Houston traffic!" At the time, I was not doing any work in Seattle; I decided to change that. I targeted a marketing effort to potential clients close to home, and over the next fifteen years I did about one-quarter of my work around Seattle. This balance was not easy to maintain, but seeking it and paying attention to it have made a difference.

Consider how this boundary applies to you. Your consulting reputation will build locally. If you are doing any work around your region, people will talk about you with people from other organizations. If you are seen favorably, you will receive an increasing number of calls from potential clients close to home. In this case, the need for local marketing is lessened because your client base is geographically concentrated, and word of mouth will do your most important marketing work for you. But can your local market support you over the long term? Can you build a life and practice working with local clients? Will they be as happy to see you ten years from now as they are today? If you are just starting out and have little business, this can seem like a ridiculous consideration. Put it aside for now and come back to it in a few years.

Work and conferences kept me away from home five to eight nights a month for most of my career. Work seldom took my weekends, though I did find myself flying out on Sunday evening, cutting a chunk off of family time. The schedule was tolerable, except about three times a year when I had managed it poorly and overcommitted myself. Travel does have a few advantages: the uninterrupted airplane time available for reading, sleeping, working, or watching a movie, for example. Because I know what a pain travel can be, I plan to use that high-altitude time enjoyably and productively. When I manage the work boundaries, the travel boundaries usually take care of themselves. Working an average of six days a month limits my time in airports and airplanes.

Living Location Boundary

Many consultants choose not only where they go to work but where they leave from. They decide where they want to live. Where do you live? Where would you like to live? If these questions have different answers, what are the advantages of each location for you and your work? When you live close to your clients, you save untold hours of commuting. My choice to move to Seattle was for the lifestyle, not for business. The commuting time from Chicago (where I used to live) to national clients is much shorter than it is from the northwest corner of the country. Consulting offers you flexibility of location that large employers cannot. As a consultant, I need a telephone jack for my computer, a cell phone, and an airport within easy driving distance. There are thousands of places in the country that meet these criteria. For two summers I worked out of a phone booth on an island with occasional plane service. On a temporary basis, that was just fine.

If you intend to do this work for many years, think about where you would like to settle. Living where you want to live means that each day at home you have something extra to celebrate. You can pause to enjoy your surroundings, knowing that you are where you want to be. Commitment to place allows you to sink deeper roots, to invest yourself more fully than you might imagine. This investment can profoundly enhance your life and well-being; it can also be reflected in your work. Your decision about where you want to live is one of the more important ones external consulting allows, even encourages. You may not be able to act on the choice immediately, but you can begin to plan for the day you will move.

Office Location Boundary

Do you need to get away from where you live to do good work? Does wearing business attire help you work better? Do you need an office you can invite clients to? Do you need daily contact with people who do work related to your own? Are you drawn to the image of having a real office in a real office building? Would you feel like less of a consultant if you worked out of your home? Affirmative answers to two or more of those questions may mean that this section is not for you. If you aren't sure where you stand, read through my experiences and notice your reactions—your clues to what you want to do.

For those of you who are still with me, listen to these typical lines spoken over the course of one week of family visits to my home office: "Can I use your markers?" "Would you kids please stop yelling when I am on the phone!" "Where is my stapler?" "Dinner's ready!" "Could you give me a ride to work?" "Would you kids please clean up the toys in my office?" "Who spilled cocoa on my computer?" Or imagine this: you are in the middle of a telephone conversation with a client, but your daughter wants to know whether she can stay overnight with a friend . . . and she wants to know *now!* Or . . . you have a report to finish before the FedEx pickup, and you were just told that the garbage is overflowing, there isn't a clean towel in the house, and the cat just threw up on the rug!

This is life with a family and a home office. All of it contributes to why I have always had my office in my home. There is no escaping it: you are at home—and you are at work. Both are true much of the time. For me, all of this creates perspective and balance. The daughter, the report, the cat, the garbage, and the laundry are all part of life. And I find life richer for having them in close proximity rather than antiseptically distant. One of the reasons I have my office at home is so I can face these real and conflicting priorities. To have one part of your mind absorbing a client's problem and another part absorbing a child's problem—that's perspective! At least it is the *opportunity* for perspective; it can also just be maddening. You will decide how you will deal with it.

As long as you have your office at home and other people or animals around, you will have many of these kinds of "opportunities." I started my practice in my basement with a hollow-core door on sawhorses as my desk. I began working at home out of necessity; I continued out of choice. Because there is only a wall separating home and office, I have to manage the boundary between them.

With practice, it has become much more a pleasure than a pain. My family knows more about my work because they see me work. I know more about the family because I am here a great deal of the time. I am available if needed to help with homework, to talk, to fix dinner, or to deal with an emergency. I can come and go from work easily. My wife and I often have time together. My family is emotionally closer because of my physical closeness. Family life puts my work in perspective, giving me a better sense of how important or unimportant my various projects are. I often get to go to work in my pajamas, do work I love, and make money. It is so comfortable to be able to begin work without going through a grooming and dressing ritual. And many of these pleasures have increased as three children became three adults and moved on to homes of their own.

And the pains of working at home? For me, most of them came with having school-age kids. When your children are young and you are the only adult at home, it is almost impossible to maintain a span of attention and keep track of the kids. Family members do not always respect the importance of your work to you. It can be very tiring to work all day and prepare meals and take care of other family needs. Another pain is that the rest of the family will likely adopt "your" work space; your children may discover that your office is a great place for a slumber party. Everyone will see your office equipment as theirs—for instance, when you and your son each have reports due tomorrow, and there is only one computer. And for those consultants planning on expanding their business, adding more people, equipment, and inventory can be difficult to do at home.

Even as I am writing about these "pains," I am saying to myself that they are not so bad. We manage them. And we all understand and appreciate each other much more. I just took a short break from writing to go into the house and get a cup of coffee. I have to go outside to get from one "zone" to the other. I noticed some new weeds taking over a corner of the garden. I stopped, pulled a few, then a few more. Twenty minutes later I finished, got my coffee, and am now back at the keyboard. This is a good example of what happens when you work at home. I have come to expect interruptions—either of my own making or of other people's. The result is perspective and considerably less expense. If you lease an office, you have to work at least a day or two a month just to support the costs.

Here are a few details about what helps a home office work better.

- Separate your physical work space with walls or a screen or an electric fence.
- Locate that space a little out of the way from other parts of your life—upstairs, around the corner, in the next room, or down the hall—so that people don't pass by frequently.
- If you put your office in your kitchen, you will live on snacks and frozen dinners. If you put your office in your living room, you will have friends over less often.
- Have a business telephone that can be answered only in your office; if possible, don't have a home telephone in the office.
- Keep all of your work stuff in your office space. Do not make common living space—such as the dining room table—into work space, because others living there may

not respect it. Your files, books, checks, and work will
be damaged or will disappear.

- Put your office in your bedroom and you will work
twenty-four hours a day.
- Make sure you have quiet, fresh air, and good light.
- Talk with the people you live with about your office
space, how you want it treated, and how you want to
work. Remind them that if you do not get your work
done, you do not get paid, and the store will repossess
the TV.

Choosing your work, with whom you work, how much
you work, your fees, where you work, where you live, and
where you have your office—all these boundaries are
operating at once. You may not have thought of some of
these as choices, but you will choose, outlining the edges
of your practice. Your clarity about what is inside and outside your practice will help you focus your effort where it
belongs. You will be a more powerful consultant when
you know what you are and are not. Well-defined boundaries remove clutter from your life and allow you to do
better work.

Managing
Your Calendar

This chapter is about time: where your time is going and your attempts to control it. Clients come to you with *their* calendars in hand, not yours. That is the consultant's reality. You can do something to control your calendar, but you will choose to do so only if there is something more important going on in your life. Otherwise, clients rule! To grow simultaneously as a business, as a consultant, and as an individual will require your constant attention to your time. Achieving lofty goals requires attending to the details of your calendar.

When work is plentiful, it is too easy to work intensely on what is in front of you, putting off friends and family who want your time, using the rationale that the work is here today and may be gone tomorrow. I have watched consultants do that and tell themselves that for years. Their patterns of overwork tell me that something else is going on, and it has more to do with their unexamined concerns than with the work coming their way. Years of grabbing every bit of work they can has consequences in the rest of their lives. They become a function of the marketplace because they see themselves that way. With this perspective come fewer options and more compulsion. My experience has shown that it doesn't have to be that way.

Achieving Balance Within Work: An Exploration

Balancing work within your life is a primary consideration, but there is also the matter of balancing the different kinds of work you do. For those readers who feel fortunate to have any work at all, this may seem like a premature concern. Those who have consulted for longer will know what I am talking about. Work that thrilled you years ago can become ho-hum. You find yourself attracted to new work but with no time to do it. In the example that follows, I was struggling with moving from doing too much training to doing more organizational consulting. Your struggle for balance will be different, but you can still work with the process I used. I have used my own numbers in the chart shown here; adapt its left-most column to your work.

Main Elements	First Year	Second Year	Third Year	Fourth Year
Consulting				
Coaching				
Training				
Speaking				
Total days				

1. Begin by looking at the main categories of the work you do. As you can see in the chart, my work falls into four categories: consulting to organizations, coaching executives,

training managers, and public speaking. These elements generate almost all of my income and take almost all of my work time. If you were to divide your work into its few main parts, what would those be? List them down your left-hand column.

As you do this, think only about the work you do that puts money in your pocket. Put aside for now your administrative work, your marketing and sales work, the non-income-generating work you do in the community, and the conferences you attend. All that is important, too, and must be supported by the core elements of your income-generating work. Right now, we want to look at what you do to earn your living.

2. How many days a year do you currently work? How do you currently invest those days to generate income? If the elements in step one make up 100 percent of your money-making time, what percentage goes to each? In my own case, the first year, I was working about 100 days. As the next chart shows, most of that time, about 80 percent, went to training. About 5 percent went to consulting, another 5 percent to coaching, and about 10 percent to speaking. Do the same rough calculation. Do not guess; go back through your calendar to see where your time really goes. Put your numbers in the first-year column.

Main Elements	First Year	Second Year	Third Year	Fourth Year
Consulting	5%			
Coaching	5%			
Training	80%			
Speaking	10%			
Total days	100			

3. Now that you have a sense of how you are using yourself, it is time to look ahead to how you would like to

be using yourself. What would you like the main elements of your paid work to be over each of the next three years? Perhaps there is something that you want to drop or add or alter. For example, when I started consulting, I was training managers almost to the exclusion of consulting, coaching, and speaking. I wanted to build these latter three elements into my work, and set about doing so. When you have identified the main elements you want in your next year of working, what percentage of your time would go into each? Using the same exercise you did with your present real work, build the work mix you would like to have over the next three years. When I brought all this together for myself, it looked like this.

Main Elements	First Year	Second Year	Third Year	Fourth Year
Consulting	5%	25%	50%	70%
Coaching	5%	5%	10%	10%
Training	80%	60%	30%	10%
Speaking	10%	10%	10%	10%
Total days	100	90	80	70

I will not go into the reasons behind my choices right now, but you can see my dramatic movement. Over four years, I significantly shifted both the content and the quantity of my paid work. Your projections represent your personal goals and values. If you know what you want and can express it in tangible terms, you will more likely do something about it.

These three steps help me think about what I am doing and what I want to do. The thinking that goes into this exercise is more valuable than the numbers that come out. After working through the steps and developing the preceding chart, I paid attention to the commitments I was making. I turned down the opportunity to do over twenty days of management training for an organization because it did not fit with my plans; it involved too much training and too much with one client. And I noticed that my best coaching client was going through a merger that I was unlikely to survive, so I was then more receptive to new coaching opportunities. In my consulting work, an associate asked me to help him with a large project, adding to my consulting days. This little chart helped me take a more proactive stance in my work. Think about your balance, your chart, your intentions, and what you could do to put your projections into action.

Slippery Success Indicators: Tracking Your Time

From my earliest days in this work, I wanted to know how I was doing. If I couldn't get the rest of the world to tell me, I could at least keep track for myself. I used my computer to create a simple spreadsheet. It allowed me to track my work, client by client; it gave me the reassurance I needed that I was doing fine—or not doing fine. It reminded me of how I was doing against my time and money goals for the year. I was alternately reassured and alarmed when looking over the actual numbers, the time and money for each client, all on one spreadsheet page. Yes, it did take some time to maintain, but doing so took me back to the vital numbers. I could see at a glance my solid prospects, the days worked, the days contracted for, and how much money I had made. It was terrific!

When I had the bugs worked out of it, I turned the spreadsheet over to a part-time employee and full-time family member. I sent him little slips of paper with what to enter on the spreadsheet and where the information should go. And he sent me back . . . nothing! So I sent him more little slips of paper with even clearer instructions. Still nothing. The spreadsheet fell out-of-date, became useless, and died. I got angry. My part-time employee persisted in his lack of concern and performance. Then he returned to his role as full-time family member. I was left with no document, no automatic totals, and my anxiety.

Six months later: I am in the bathroom looking into the bottom left-hand drawer beside the sink. I see soap. Lots of soap. Little bars of soap with hotels' names on them. There must be fifteen little bars of soap. I start thinking about where they came from. I can tell from the number of bars that I have been traveling a lot lately and that I have been working for clients who put me in some very nice hotels from which I take the soap—just as the hotel management planned. Some Neutrogena; some wonderful black soap in a lovely little container. Not much Ivory. The soap drawer looks good today! And my feelings about the amount of work I have and my bank account are pretty good too. Hmmm . . . I begin to notice a possible correlation between the amount and type of soap I am collecting and the amount and type of work I am doing. I am comforted.

Six months later, same scene: I am looking into the soap drawer, and it is practically empty! All the good soap has been used up! I am down to a little broken bar of Camay with a wrapper that defies opening. A light begins to dawn. Could it be? I look at my calendar. Over recent months, it looks almost as bare as the soap drawer. I look at my checking account, and it is pretty bare too. I haven't been doing much work over the last month or so. Ah-ha! There is a direct relationship between the amount and type of soap in my drawer, the amount and type of work in my calendar, and the balance in my checking account!

I never did reactivate my electronic spreadsheet. My soap drawer doesn't tell me everything, but it does signal that something is going on. I view it as a clean and informative indicator of what will be happening in my refrigerator. Do not overcomplicate your consulting practice and your life with financial and business planning methods that are larger or more complex than you need. Seek simplicity in those core business processes you use; it takes time to maintain them. Wonderful software packages are available to help you analyze everything you do not need to know; choose carefully.

I brought, and still bring, considerable financial anxiety to my work. At first, I thought it was related to my lack of money (or soap). Yet sometimes when I have lots of money, I am worried; and at other times, when I have little, I am not. Eventually I saw the pattern: I need to fret about money at least four times a year, whether I have any or not! The roots of this worry are probably somewhere back in my childhood, unrelated to my current financial circumstances. What about you? How do you meet your need for good, solid business information? Do you have a system—spreadsheet or soap—that relieves your anxieties?

Making Money

*L*ike most consultants, I hesitate before putting a financial value on my services. It's hard to know what to charge. When I was new to this work, my ignorance reinforced my insecurity and deepened my fear that nobody would pay me anything! Then there was the real problem of just stating my fee to a prospective client: "My d-d-d-daily f-f-f-fee is t-t-t-t-twelve h-h-h-h-hundred d-d-d-dollars"—while maintaining steady, confident eye contact. Even now, with many fee discussions behind me, I still hesitate before talking about fees, especially when raising my fee with old clients.

In this chapter, we will talk about money: what it means, how much you want, and ways of getting it. It will help you think about how money is, and is not, significant in what you do and who you are. We will explore distinctions between what you need and what you want, related to what you are worth. We will consider alternatives *for* getting money as well as alternatives *to* getting money. As we go along, notice your reactions to this chapter on money. Notice your expectations, your readiness to deal with the subject.

The Meaning of Money

I think about money often. Too often. And in thinking about it, in giving it time, I increase its importance. The money mirror reflects back whatever we want from it. Having lots of it can mean status, success, power, sex appeal, self-esteem, security, safety, ego, recognition, reward. Having little can mean the opposite. Money has the meaning we assign to it, and its meaning is more ambiguous because we can trade it in for things we value. When you look at money, what do you see in it? What does it mean to you? Mentally note six words or phrases that you first associate with money. When you think about the money you get or want from consulting, what does that money mean to you? How important is money to the work you do? Are you consulting primarily for the money? Would you consult even if you were not paid for it? Or even if you were paid less? All these questions figure in determining your fees and in contracting with clients. Clients will sense money's importance to you, which suggests that you ought to think about it first.

Years ago I overheard a cocktail party conversation between a consultant and a potential client. The client was explaining her situation and getting a few ideas from the consultant. Less than ten minutes into the conversation, the consultant said, "I cannot talk to you any further about this matter without starting my meter." It took less than a minute for the potential client to leave, and I have no doubt about what she concluded was this consultant's primary motivation.

The Consequences of Money

Whether you have it or not, money has consequences. Money is neutral in moral value; its goodness or badness depends on how you see it and use it. Having money can corrupt you—as can not having it. Money is spoken of as a necessary evil, or as the root of all evil, but these aphorisms do not necessarily apply to those green bills in your wallet. Money may serve greed, selfishness, anxiety, generosity, love, or charity; we who have or want money decide. You can choose to see the positive or negative potential of money in your life. Face the struggles that come with having it and using it well. With money or without it, you will have to deal with the consequences of your financial state. Do not make negative assumptions about money; do incline yourself toward the possibilities that money might offer. Don't assume that it is good or bad. See it as a resource that you can use to serve your purposes.

One consequence of money relates to your freedom and control. Consider how money now controls you and how it gives you freedom. For example, U.S. citizens are carrying more credit card debt per capita than ever before in our history. Millions of high credit card balances are reducing the financial options of millions of individuals. Forget good and bad; when we carry high personal debt, we have fewer choices.

A solid financial foundation serves your consulting practice in many ways. With money in the bank, you can more readily choose the work you want to do. Without money, you are apt to take whatever comes along, plans be damned. With more financial security, you can look into a client's true needs; with less financial security, you might recommend your services because you need the money— at least that has been true for me. When I need work, I am tempted to serve my self-interest first rather than the client's needs. I am not proud of the times I have taken on or created work that served me and cost the client. I do recognize that I have done it, and having this awareness is a necessary step before taking action.

Living Below Your Means

One of the best things you can do to maintain your emotional and mental balance is to live below your means. Spend less than you earn. If you are currently spending every dollar (and more) and are unhappy, you can't escape this state until you create savings that provide you with options now and later in life. Knowing you have something tucked away makes you less dependent on your clients; you will take risks more readily when you know that your credit card company is not dogging you to get your minimum payment in. You will be more willing to put forth those innovative ideas that are worth consideration but might jeopardize your relationship with your client. With less at stake, you can afford the risk.

I was riding to a Chicago airport with a new manager from my client company. She asked me what she ought to do as she started this new job. I guessed that she had received a huge salary increase in moving to this company, and she acknowledged she had. I told her not to spend it, to continue to live at the level she was living at before, increasing her options. If she upgraded her spending to her new salary, she could end up owing her soul to the company store. If she couldn't afford to lose this job, she would hesitate to speak up. That same thinking applies to us consultants.

Start saving early, and you are more likely to make it a habit. You will reap larger long-term dividends. When you begin saving early in your consulting career—before you are at the height of your earning power—you won't develop spending habits that destroy your ability to save. Starting a savings program at age forty-five is much harder than starting at age thirty. The older person is beyond his formative years; the younger person is still shaping her financial habits. The forty-five-year-old has half the time left to reach the same goals as the thirty-year-old.

Keep your options open by managing your finances well. You may be the most wonderful consultant in the world, but if you do not manage funds well, you will find your choices constantly preempted by your financial weaknesses. Thousands of decisions will be affected by the financial base you build. Whether you are receiving it or paying it, recognize the impact of compound interest. Get on the receiving side of the ledger and stay there. A solid financial base gives you options, options offer choice, and choice is personal power.

Setting Fees: An Exploration

We consultants struggling with money frequently visit questions in four areas: what we are worth, what we can get, what we need, and what we want—different but related considerations. We will explore each of these areas and engage you in all four varieties of concern. Follow the process whether you are considering becoming a consultant, are a new consultant, or have been consulting for many years; the process will help your thinking. It is based on the exploration my wife and I did before I chose to be a consultant. As I explain what we did, run a parallel set of calculations for yourself.

There were two levels of financial need that especially concerned us: what we had to have to barely get by—a subsistence level—and what we needed so as to live in "reasonable comfort." The "barely get by" level could work for many months but would not be sustainable over years. The "reasonable comfort" level was much less than we wanted to have, but a level my family could live with indefinitely. With that backdrop . . .

1. *Calculating the "barely get by," subsistence level.* If money was really tight, how little could we get by on without missing any payments that would take away the house, the car, the children, the electricity, or the telephone? We calculated that we needed $1,500 a month ($18,000 a year) to barely get by—yes, this was years ago! We could continue in this uncomfortable state for six to twelve months, but certainly not for years. If this was the best we could do, consulting would not be worth it. Take a few minutes to do a rough calculation for yourself.

2. *Calculating the "reasonable comfort" level.* How much did we need to live comfortably and feel that the move to consulting was worth it from a family, personal, and professional standpoint—at a level we knew we could continue indefinitely? This included small savings, a family vacation, and better insurance. We calculated that $3,000 per month ($36,000 per year) would provide reasonable comfort for years—though this would fall far short of what we wanted to have. What would you require for reasonable comfort?

3. *Determining how many days a year I wanted to work.* This consideration was partly financial, partly lifestyle. We concluded that working one hundred paid days a year

would bring the kind of balance in our lives and family that we were looking for. Think about this carefully before you decide; consider what is best for you in terms of both money and your life as a whole.

4. *Determining what my daily fees had to be.* By dividing $18,000 and $36,000 by one hundred, we calculated that my fees needed to be at least $180 per day to subsist and $360 per day to be reasonably comfortable. What would your range be?

5. *Looking in the marketplace.* What could I get out there? I interviewed a dozen consultants and clients, I assessed my own experience, I considered our needs, and I considered what I was ready to ask for. I decided I wanted $400 per day. That calculates out as about four or five paid days a month to meet our subsistence-level needs. I was certain I could find that much work. It would mean an average of nine days a month of actual, paid work to be comfortable. That felt scary to me, a guy who had been regularly showing up at the corporate pay window for fourteen years. But I thought it was worth trying. It meant that if I could meet my paid work goals, I would still have plenty of time for marketing, family, administrative work, and friends. So we decided on $400 per day. What does the marketplace tell you? What would your fees be? I know that you might calculate them on quite a different basis, but in the end you have to match your potential sources of income with your needs.

You may have noticed that these five steps leave out something essential: the results of your consulting efforts, what you contribute to your client organizations. That is a paramount—and quite different—consideration. Here we are talking about the needs you must meet to survive. You will not prosper as a consultant if you charge fees that do not allow you to sustain yourself. This makes sense, but I have heard a number of consultants say (1) "I am so busy!!" (2) "I can't continue doing this work if I don't raise my fees," and (3) "I am afraid that if I raise my fees, I'll lose my clients." Consultants using this kind of thinking are like retailers selling below cost and trying to make up the loss with high volume! It's a good way to be temporarily popular, but they will end up underpaid burnouts.

Low Needs and High Discipline

One other consideration: the simple math described in the preceding section succeeds only when you keep your subsistence needs low—low enough that you can meet them with ease and make such wonderful contributions to clients that you attract others willing to pay higher fees. Begin by holding down your needs; work up to billing out at higher rates. Neither early greed nor a high need to acquire things serves you well.

When I began consulting, I needed four or five paid days each month to cover our subsistence-level needs. A combination of keeping needs low and raising fees allowed me to gradually reduce those required monthly days to three, then two, then one. Of course, I was working much more than these minimums, but knowing how few days it took to cover our basic monthly needs gave me peace of mind.

Those early decisions served me and my family well. Our modest expectations were readily met, and that was exciting. By intentionally limiting my work, I averaged seventy-three paid days a year. This took some skill, considerable discipline, clear intentions, and good fortune. There were times when I slipped off track, when I let my anxieties speak rather than my plan, or when I overspent and underearned. The negative consequences of such slips reminded me of what was really important and helped me return to the path I had charted. I am describing, not prescribing, my approach. I do not know what will work for you, but I believe that creating your business, your life, and your future requires careful and consistent attention.

What You Charge and What You Are Worth

I do not know my absolute worth to my clients. My work is worth something, but there is no accurate way of determining that worth. The marketplace tells me something, but that does not satisfy me. I find it freeing to acknowledge that I don't know what my work is actually worth and neither do my clients. I do know how much I want; my clients know how much they are willing to pay. We talk and agree.

My work is of value, but the amount of money I am paid is what I agree to. The expertise I bring, how I use it, how hard I work, how much I actually contribute—none of these important factors has much to do with what I get paid. The marketplace decides my pay much more than any of these work-related factors. Consider how much nurses are paid . . . and rock stars . . . and teachers . . . and ball players . . . and stay-at-home parents . . . and consultants. This is not about justice; this is about the marketplace.

We are not talking about what you and I are worth; we are talking about what you and I can get. The way you decide what to charge and the way other people decide what to pay you have little to do with your expertise or experience or the contribution you are making in the world. Your ultimate value as a consultant or as a human being is not put on the line in this negotiation; what you are paid is a function of the marketplace, a mechanism not noted for its contemplation of life's meaning.

You can't put a financial value on who you are, so don't mix up your struggles about personal worth with your efforts to sell your services. If you insist on struggling, put your energies into figuring out what you can get in the marketplace for your work. What are clients paying others for work similar to the work you want to do? Ask other consultants; check the Internet; ask clients. Most important of all, ask yourself what you want clients to pay you.

This discussion brings to mind two consultant friends of mine. One, whose expertise I respect highly, has been struggling to establish himself as a consultant for at least ten years. The other is a lot of fun to be with, but I see his expertise as limited and narrow. Yet clients hire him back again and again—and for lots of money! If you hold expertise as the standard, these two examples do not make sense.

How do you handle that "money moment" in your negotiations? Tell the client what you want. "I want $50 a day for this work." "I want $5,000 a day to do this work." Whatever you plan to say, look them in the eye, tell them what you want, and be quiet. Do not apologize or make excuses; just say it. To make this easier, initiate the subject; don't wait for the client to ask, perhaps finding you unprepared. Deal with the subject when you choose to. Tell your clients how much you want rather than what you charge. For example, I feel stronger saying to an old client, "Starting the first of the year, I want $900 a day for my work with you" than I do saying, "My fee goes up January first; I will be billing clients $900 a day." The "I want . . ." statement is stronger for me because it is true; I do want to raise my fee. It is easier for me to say so directly without putting it forth as an accomplished fact.

Years ago I approached a client about raising my fees 50 percent. There were many reasons I could make up, but most of all I wanted more and thought I deserved it. When I told him what I wanted, he asked why he ought to pay half again as much for me tomorrow as he was paying for me today. I thought long and carefully before saying, "Damned if I know, but that's what I want!" For similar reasons, he met my want. Damned if any of us know! Fees are a matter determined by some dynamic among the marketplace, your work, yourself, and your client. When you tell clients what you want, it only makes sense that they can tell you what they want. And maybe they do not want to give you what you want. That's OK. You don't always get what you want. And it won't be because you are wrong. You may be disappointed, but you are not wrong. And . . . you may just get what you want!

There are many ways of being paid. I am usually paid a daily fee, plus expenses. Elaine Biech's book *The Business of Consulting* elaborates on your many alternatives. For me, being paid a daily rate simplifies the financial side of working with clients. They know that if I am working for them, the meter is running. It is easy for us to track. This arrangement has the advantage of not narrowing our focus to just the immediate project. We can go where the work takes us, based on the needs of the organization. There is room for innovation. I frequently work on projects that are defined only broadly in the beginning; the client and I do not know what the outcomes will be at that point. A daily fee fits well with this kind of exploratory work.

There are downsides to this way. First, per diem pays for activity, not results. Second, I do not share in any financial gains created in the organization through my work. Third, I make money only when I am working. There are alternatives for making money whereby the amount is not precisely related to effort invested. On per diem you only make money while you are awake; other approaches allow you to make money while you sleep. For example, if you run a website loaded with content your paying subscribers love, they will be paying you whether you are there or not.

Negotiating Fees

I discourage you from going in to negotiate fees with a client. I encourage you to figure out what you want and ask for it. When you have decided what and how you are going to charge your clients for your services, stick to it. Do not try to adapt your fees to each client who comes along. Charge the same fee for the same service to clients in the same geographic area. Try to hold on to this fee structure for at least one year.

Instead of negotiating fees, negotiate the work to be done. When a client is concerned about your fees being too high, discuss what work needs doing and how much money the client is willing to pay to get it done. In the process, you can usually find ways that meet both parties' financial needs. Perhaps a piece of the work can be left out, or data can be gathered from fewer rather than more people, or a report may include less than you originally intended. Rather than lowering your fee, another approach is to give clients some time. For example, if the project will take five days and you charge $1,000 a day, but the clients have only $4,000, bill them for four days at $1,000 per day and give them the fifth day for nothing. This way you get the work, they get their work done, you are seen as generous, they owe you, and you have not reduced your fees. A variation on this approach would be to take the same actions but not tell the clients that it took you five days instead of four.

Consistent Fees

An important reason to hold to a consistent fee is to be fair to your other clients. How fair are you being to them if you are willing to do similar work for less money across town? Granted, you deal with them separately, and each contract is agreed to by each client, so no one is being cheated. But I am guessing that you will feel better knowing that you are consistent in a way that is easily understood by everyone. Consistency does not mean that you have only one fee; it means that you are consistent in the fees you have. For example, I charge significantly more for work out of town than I do for work in town. I also charge more for training groups than I do for consulting to individuals. And I charge in yet another way for speeches to conferences or corporations.

Do not track and bill your work so tightly that you have to worry about every minute you are working and whether you are being paid for it. Keep your attention on your work by reducing worries about money. If you can, charge clients enough that you are comfortable working extra time for them. As a rule, when I am in doubt about whether to charge for time worked, I do not charge.

Setting fees still tests me; I have more on the line than I acknowledge. And this hidden unease offers me clues to my vulnerability and my doubts about my self-worth.

When I hear that another consultant is charging much more than I, my old questions about my value and my fees return. If certain clients indicate that they are paying a lot of money for me, I start wondering about what I am doing for them, if I might do more, if I am overcharging them. These doubts and fears have gone on for years; I can see the pattern. It's not a matter of getting rid of them but of acknowledging and managing them.

I detailed my own struggles with money and work in the hope of stirring your thoughts and feelings. As you finish this chapter, what points or issues are important to you?

Part Two

The Clients

Why Clients Hire You

$\mathcal{W}$hat attracts clients to you time after time? Consider the question. Do you have ready answers? Would your answers sort you out from all the other consultants available to your clients? I have thought about these questions; I will share my answers here, but it is your answers that are most important. What does client after client say about you? Early in your practice, the answers to these questions are less apparent, less important, and probably less accurate. You are still trying to figure out who you are! But with time, good clients, and personal reflection, you will know more about what attracts clients to you.

I asked twenty independent consultants who had been in business at least ten years what kept clients coming back to them for years—at least five years. The words I often heard in those interviews included the following:

Accomplishment	Purpose	Contribution
Challenge	Perspective	Process
Partnership	Expertise	Hardship
Fun	Learning	Insight
Motivation	Authenticity	Life
Contract	Appreciation	Loyalty
Friendship	Openness	Connection

Compare their answers to your own; you may want to add to the list. My answers are among those listed here. Clients come back to me time after time because of my combination of five "abilities": I offer contribution, expertise, perspective, authenticity, and friendship. Your answers may be different. Each attribute helps make my work important to my life. In combination they define much of what I stand for as a consultant. I think clients keep working with me because they too value these abilities—whether they know it or not.

This chapter and the next discuss the five abilities I have identified as crucial to my work; here we will look at contribution, expertise, and perspective. All three are embedded in the work itself: accomplishing something at work, having the talent to help at work, and offering alternative ways of seeing the work. The remaining two abilities, authenticity and friendship, have more to do with relationships surrounding the work; they will be discussed in the next chapter.

Contribution

Clients expect to be better off after we leave than they were before we arrived. The net difference is our contribution. Well, speaking more modestly, not *all* that happens is because of us, but we help. Many clients will proclaim that our contribution is the *entire* reason they keep us around. I don't believe it, but I ignore their point at my own peril. I think the other elements (perspective, authenticity, expertise, and friendship) are also important in explaining why they keep using you and me, even when contribution is temporarily lacking. I once told a client that I hadn't really accomplished much lately and that I suspected he was keeping me around because he liked me. He told me that I was wrong and that he was patient. So I may be as authentic as hell, I may have expertise running out of my attaché case, I may provide clients with forty-seven perspectives, and I may be the best friend they could ever have—but if we don't get something done together, the work is in trouble!

Contribution is the net positive difference you help make for your client organization. It may be a successful meeting today, a successful project next month, a successful series of efforts that lead to results in three years. Contributions must be both realized and recognized. It is not enough to do "it," whatever "it" is; key people have to know about it if you want to keep working there. Sometimes we must point out and emphasize: "Look at what we have done together today," or "I feel proud of what we have accomplished over the last year," or "You people have done one terrific job of bringing this dream to reality!" Of course, you too have to realize how you have helped. I have done work that the clients were happy with but that I was unhappy with. This is not the pattern I want to establish. It is not enough that clients see the contribution. I must see it too.

Build patterns of recognized contribution. Pay attention to even the small successes you and the client accomplish together. Do not take your contributions for granted. When you face the setbacks that invariably come with long and difficult projects, you will be able to deal with these setbacks in the context of a larger, established pattern of contribution.

Be conscious of what you contributed within the larger accomplishment. Although not always easy to identify, this has much to do with why you continue to be used by this client. Knowing what you have been bringing to the work suggests how you might be used next, building on your demonstrated contribution. If your recent work didn't make that much difference, maybe the client is ready to work without you, or maybe you need to find new ways of contributing.

To recognize what they have accomplished, clients often need help, for at least two reasons. First, you may have helped them do something they have never done before, so when change occurs, they are not experienced enough to recognize what they have accomplished. Second, they are so busy solving new problems that they may not stop to look back at their progress. Helping our client partners celebrate what they have done brings new learning and new energy to the work we are doing together.

In one meeting with forty middle managers, we were about to discuss progress on a project we had been pursuing for six months. Before the meeting, our lunchtime conversation had centered on our disappointment about how little had been accomplished. Now in the meeting, the manager asked small groups to discuss and list what had happened since the start of this change effort. Soon groups were buzzing with discussion and in twenty minutes had listed five pages of actions they attributed to the change effort. We were all amazed at what had been accomplished. And without the manager's request, we would not have known. I repeat: contributions must be realized and recognized.

Expertise

Many clients cite my expertise as the main reason they are using me. I don't agree. Expertise is essential but not the reason they come back again and again. They say expertise first because it is easier to talk about than the real reasons they keep asking me back. Expertise still deserves to be near the top of the list of what I offer because it is an essential "given." We must offer abilities that clients need, use, and value. We cannot get by on being friendly and authentic; we have to bring and apply talent clients see as affecting outcomes positively. And our expertise must involve something they don't know how to do, don't have time to do, are not in the position to do, or don't want to do. Find out which of these reasons is behind their interest in you. Their reason affects what working relationship you have with them: you and your clients may be codesigners, teacher and learners, consultant and guides, or coworkers.

Clients often deal with me as if I have expertise that does not exist anywhere in the organization. That is seldom true. Most often, there are abilities hanging around the halls and cubicles that no one has bothered to discover and put to work. I count on that being true, because if it weren't, the organization would not be able to bring about the changes it decides it wants. So from early in the consulting relationship, I am trying to find out how my expertise fits with expertise present in the organization. I plan to use their expertise as this project moves forward; I do not want to increase dependence on me.

Clients often assign me a level and type of expertise that exceeds or is different from what I actually possess. They do this in their need for the consultant and the project to be important, and my ego supports this because it loves attention and power. But I have to watch out for what this inflation does to my effectiveness. For example, the client and I can mutually conspire to make me too much the leader on projects, or to do too much of the work myself. Why? Because no one is better qualified, of course. See the trap?

Perspective

First, an example. Having spent my early career as a trainer, I was disposed to think of organization problems as training problems—especially in the realm of management behavior or interpersonal behavior. I "knew" that if someone was not doing something very well, it was because he or she needed training. And of course I was a trainer, so wasn't that nice for both of us? Not surprisingly, now that I don't do much training anymore, I see these situations differently. More accurately: I see situations differently now, so I don't do much training anymore. I have learned, my perspective has changed, I see the world differently.

In my work, it is most important that I bring clients new perspective. I help them see their world in new ways; with their new vision, new alternatives suggest themselves. Their new views suggest actions that were literally inconceivable in their old view. Take the case of Tom . . .

Tom and I had been working for two years on a variety of projects, resulting in considerable mutual respect and trust. Tom's outstanding performance led to the offer of a new position at another location. He accepted the promotion without thinking about it and immediately felt very uneasy. He did not want to move, but knew that you "always" accept promotions. He had accepted six in eight years, moving his family every time. Within his corporate work perspective, acceptance was the only alternative available to him—regardless of how uneasy he might feel. He felt trapped.

One month later, Tom felt released from his trap. More than that, he felt solid, relieved, even expansive. What had happened? In the interim, Tom and his wife and children spent hours talking about the effect the move would have on them. Tom saw the importance of keeping the children in their present schools with their friends. He heard about the toll previous moves had taken on his wife, her life, and their relationship. They spent time discussing how they wanted to live their lives; they envisioned their future together. They put those dreams up against moving to work in another city for more money. As they considered his work in a larger life perspective, new alternatives opened. Tom went back to management and reversed his earlier decision. He explained why, saying he would live with the consequences. Everyone was surprisingly understanding, making Tom's action easier for him. He felt terrific because he had acted in his and his family's best interests, and in the process confirmed his family's importance to him. It could have turned out much differently and not so well.

Tom did the shifting, and I accompanied and guided him. As a consultant, I reinforced what he was thinking about. I offered ideas on how he might think about his dilemma differently. I suggested ways for him to talk with his family. And I joined him in celebrating his decision. Tom's shift in perspective opened new alternatives to him. I try to do this kind of work with all my clients, because I believe that the new perspective and new insight lead to new options. I assume my clients have skills they are not putting to use right now because they cannot see how those skills would be helpful. Perspective more than skill is what they lack. Like all of us, they get trapped and trap themselves in seeing the world from only one point of view; within that viewpoint they can find few alternative actions—and none that are satisfying to them.

When clients explain their problem to me, I ask lots of questions. I ask what they have tried, and usually find that they have tried "everything." I suggest alternatives, and they tell me why those alternatives "won't work." Sound familiar? They are stuck. And because they are very smart people, they are very stuck people! They have figured every possible angle on this situation, and they know clearly why they cannot do anything about it except what they are doing—which is unsatisfactory.

As you might guess, I seldom say, "You need more skills to handle this." Most of the problems brought to me center on people, and "people skills" are required to deal with them. My clients often have many of the people skills they need, and they are prevented from using these skills by their point of view. They see the situation in a way that precludes their using the appropriate skills. Or they don't understand that the skills might be necessary. Or they might be afraid to use their skills because they see the consequences as negative. Or maybe they don't know when to use their skills because no one has indicated that the skills are needed.

They have all these reasons and more for withholding their abilities, all related to how they see the situation. I try to help them see the situation differently in order to free them to do what they already know how to do. I start with understanding the situation as they understand it and getting their assurance that I do understand them. Then together we open our search for other ways of seeing the situation. When we have at least one new perspective that seems to have value, we start considering what actions that view of the world might suggest. After that, we look at what it would be like for them to carry out those actions. Last of all, they decide what they really will do.

In the search for other perspectives, I seldom think, "They are not looking at this narrowly enough!" No, I do not encourage them to burrow in on their job when they have their whole life to consider, as did Tom. Broader, wider, larger life perspectives open doors and invigorate the search for options. Moving toward a life perspective for individuals or organizations leads to their empowerment. This book attempts to do this with you. Its chapters regularly ask you to lift up your head from your work to consider the life you have and the life you want to create. I do the same work with my clients.

Focusing on perspective rather than skill is especially useful to people with long experience in what they are doing. When we are newer to our work, we see ourselves as learners; we more readily accept training and guidance when we know we need it. Adding knowledge and skills to our repertoire aids our performance in our early years. Later in life and work, it is a different story. We have built up our store of abilities and experience; we expect to use it, and we expect to be respected for what we have. We are less likely to jump at the opportunity to learn more when we think we already know a great deal—even when we get stuck. But help us see the situation differently, and we will release the abilities we have that are appropriate to the situation. Life is a bit more complex than this, but you see the point. What do you bring clients in the way of new perspective?

Seven

Why Clients
Keep You

The previous chapter explored what you bring to the work itself that clients and you value. This chapter shifts our focus from the work itself to your relationship with clients, to you as a person. Not just you contributing, or you with expertise, or you offering perspective. This chapter is about your readiness to bring your true self to work. Because this is a personal chapter, I will tell you what I have done. What I have learned is not "right," but I am invested in it. I have thought deeply about it, and I encourage you to do so as well, coming to your own conclusions. This chapter is about the potential for authenticity and friendship in our work.

Authenticity

I must have the opportunity to be myself at work. Please note the subtitle of this book: *Bringing Who You Are to What You Do*. I have done work that requires me to pretend constantly, to step into a heavy and awkward costume that requires me to pretend to be another person. This is just too hard! I can imagine a threat hanging over me that could make it necessary, but only with that threat could I do it. I can imagine it, but I don't choose it. This work increases the possibility of my becoming my better self while in service to others.

Independent consultants have the opportunity to shape their business around themselves; that is a privilege less available to workers who are asked to shape themselves around an assigned role within a system, perhaps even to a machine or a process. We can pattern our little businesses to our own design. That leads to certain questions: What is my design for this little business? What is the business becoming? Who am I, and how does that show through my work? What am I becoming? How will I present myself inside and outside of work? What do I tell others about who I am and what I do? These questions link to the idea of authenticity.

Without pursuing the answers to these questions, we become entirely reactive to what's going on "out there" in the business world and lose touch with what is going on "in here" with ourselves. We will not know the answers before venturing forth, but we should know the questions and be seeking their answers. Many answers will reveal themselves as we encounter the marketplace.

Working for yourself, by yourself, requires a helluva lot of motivation! That motivation is directly linked to your authenticity: to the extent that through this work you are who you want to be, you will persevere on this path. To the extent that this work requires you to play a role that doesn't fit you, the path will be less attractive, and you will be less motivated.

The basic reason to pursue authenticity in your work is not just to be motivated; that is a valuable by-product.

The better reason is that there is nothing more important to do in this life than to become yourself. And you can do that by being an authentic consultant. When you intend to become yourself through your work, you eliminate a lot of complications. You don't have to remember what role you are trying to play, because you are being yourself. You can forget about how you should behave at work and at home because there is no difference in the perspective you bring to each place. You don't have to tell small lies to cause people to think you are someone you are not. You don't have to pretend, invent, fake, or feign interest. There is nothing to make up; there is no posturing to do. Your life is simplified by your authenticity.

You can use your work experiences to hone your understanding of what it means to be authentic. For example, while giving my consulting time to a local nonprofit, I found myself being unusually blunt with the client. My bluntness was particularly effective, partly because it was so clear. I was not tiptoeing around the issues; I was not worried about whether the client would hire me again. I later realized that I was behaving differently because I was not being paid to do the work. I learned something about what I withhold from my paying clients for fear of losing their friendship, the work, and my reputation. My success with the volunteer work caused me to think that I might also have been withholding my effectiveness from paying clients. That experience moved me a notch closer to authenticity with other clients.

Friendship

Put aside your role as a consultant for a minute and think about what you want from your friends. List a handful of statements, each beginning with "I want . . ." When you have collected your wants, read my statements: I want to be myself, and I want people to accept me as I am. I want my friends to tell me why they like me, as well as how I get on their nerves. I want to be able to do risky, even silly, things with my friends, knowing that they will accept my behavior. I want to be able to talk about what is important to me and to be taken seriously. I want to work and play with friends, accomplish things, reach goals shoulder to shoulder, and enjoy those accomplishments together. I want to be able to talk with friends about my concerns, knowing that they will support me. I want my friends to be comfortable with me, to talk, to take risks, to share concerns, to be serious, and generally to want to work and play with me.

My guess is that your list and mine are similar enough that you will understand when I say that my ideal client partnerships are friendships. When I meet with a potential client, I am thinking about my potential contribution, my expertise, the perspectives I might bring, how authentic I might be, and whether this work could possibly lead to a friendship. No, it is not necessary for me to be friends with all my clients, and friendship is not my first priority, but I do think about it. I do not think we show up at work just to contribute, to do the tasks before us, to take the money, and go home. Some of us perhaps, but not many. Most of us are also looking for work that contains some of the ingredients of friendship. We know the potential that friendship has for deepening the work experience. When I think back on the work of which I have been proudest, from which I learned the most, and in which I contributed the most, friendship was involved about 80 percent of the time. And the friendship contributed to the positive results. Even now, five years after finishing my most active years as a paid consultant, I stay in touch with old clients and they with me. Within the last week, I have had at least five contacts with those old clients, even though I have not worked with them for years.

Here's the tough part: when I think about work I didn't enjoy, from which I didn't learn, or in which I didn't accomplish much, friendship was also involved some of the time. Being friendly and building friendship with clients do not guarantee success. Friendship can complicate matters significantly; I have suffered through some of those complications. But the advantages of client friendships have offset the complications that come with a few. I choose to live with those occasional complications rather than deprive myself of the richness added to my work by my client-friends. I spend many hours of my life devoted to this work, and I want those to be rich hours.

An openness to friendship with clients deepens the potential of this consulting work to contribute to life meaning. The possibility of developing friendships with your partners-in-work affects how you deal with them. It guides you toward openness, equality, naturalness, and authenticity. It causes you to look for opportunities to be with them and to do things with them, beyond just work. It can mean that you end up talking with them at all hours of the day and night. It makes it difficult to sort work from nonwork.

Becoming friends with clients also removes some advantages of the more formal client-consultant relationship that I sometimes value. I miss being set apart, being treated as special because of my expertise. I lose the ability to control my professional image of being highly knowledgeable, always having good ideas, and knowing what to do next. As I become closer with the client, they forget that I am different, expert, special! Sometimes they wonder why they are paying me so much money when I am so ordinary, not much different from them. And I lose my objectivity when I get close with the people as well as the issues of the organization. As I work there longer, I become more a part of the issues and less an observer of them. When clients feel familiar with me, they call me at home to talk about work and personal problems, and this cuts into other personal time. So there are losses as the clients find out who I really am—but most of what is lost is pretense and image.

Clients have mentioned that they are not used to having consultants treat them as friends. Many of them like this and keep using me. Our friendship carries beyond the present project or even their present organization; they call as they move into new positions in new organizations. I think this is a primary explanation for the number of clients I have worked with for five years or more. These client friendships have greatly reduced the time I have spent seeking new clients. I know this only by looking back on my experience; it was not intentional. Of course there have been many clients who did not like my approach. They moved on to seek consultants who fit better with what they wanted.

My years of talking with consultants about friendship with clients has stirred much discussion and yielded no unanimous conclusions. You should therefore think of friendship with clients as an option for you, not a prescription.

Eight

Building Trust with Clients

We have some compelling, practical reasons to build trust with our clients. As consultants, we are usually there to change something. Change requires risk taking. Risk taking requires trust. For there to be trust, there must be a relationship. No, they do not necessarily develop in that sequence, but they do develop, or you pay the consequences. So even if you did not feel naturally inclined to develop deeper partnership with your clients, you can see how it could make sense to do so.

Clients worry about working with us. They worry that if they choose to work with us, they could incur costs that exceed the benefits realized. Besides investing dollars, they invest precious time and energy—and often their reputations. Our proposals ask clients to move in directions as yet undefined based on information as yet uncollected. I still recall a client's "encouraging words" whispered in my ear as we were walking into his boardroom to present a proposal: "Now don't screw this up!" Just the boost I needed at the moment. That client was invested in his success and his organization's success. Most are. They put themselves on the line with us. They often give us powers in their organization that they ordinarily reserve for themselves and a few trusted others. They know that things will be different after we begin work and that not all of those differences are predictable.

They ask themselves whether they really want to enter this relationship, with all its uncertainties. Words going through their minds might include trust, risk, control, trust, opportunity, risk, trust, concern, excitement, trust—and maybe risk. The most difficult elements of a client's decision to use a consultant are the intangible and subjective. Clients want to be willing to take the risks with us; they want to be able to trust us.

The considerations in hiring a consultant are very similar to the decisions employers make when hiring a full-time associate. Candidates are checked out for the resources and powers they bring. Their talents, abilities, and style allow their uniqueness to show, which selects them in or out of the process. The employer looks through the better applicants for fit and generally uses fit to decide. The potential employee is going through the same process. A major difference in the client-consultant process is that we consultants go through the "employment process" repeatedly every year. And we are being considered for a relatively short period of "employment." Our repeated experiences with getting "hired" can aid us in learning how to make the process go well for us and our clients.

Another analogy comes to mind: the high school dance. I see girls talking with each other along one wall and a crowd of boys across the room. The music begins, and for those who want to dance, this is the moment. Girls often wait to be asked or dance with each other. The girls are very aware of the power of the boys' position. One boy casually glances across the room, finding the girl he would like to dance with and working up the nerve to ask. After finding her, he steps out into that long, empty space that separates them, and strolls across the floor to ask her. As he begins to move across the floor, the balance of power shifts. A moment ago, he held the power to choose; now she has the choice and the power.

While the client is deciding whether to invest in me, I'm deciding whether to invest in the client. This really does go both ways—or it ought to for the partnership to be strong. I may want to dance, but does the client? The client may want to dance, but do I? We must each see the opportunity for this to work; our respective powers must balance.

The client-consultant partnership is going to be based on a good fit between the two participants. Trust and risk are key elements in creating a mutual fit. Each partner must trust; each must risk. Trust and risk depend on each other. How they affect each other is not as predictable as the fact that they do. If clients trust me, they are more willing to risk with me, and vice versa. It is almost pointless for me to encourage clients to risk if they do not yet trust me.

Clients' unwillingness to risk can be related to their degree of trust in me or to perceptions of what is happening in the organization. Both deserve attention. The former is easier to act on because I am part of the difficulty. Repair work between clients and me will prepare us to take on the organization. There are other risk behaviors I pay attention to: when clients risk out of proportion to the trust relationship we have established, this clues me to the clients' desperation, foolishness, or lack of awareness. Or when clients show a pattern of resisting the size, costs, timing, or details of a project, this behavior may be a clue that they lack the trust necessary to risk.

You cannot eliminate the real risk present in change work. Building trust can make risk more acceptable, but it will not make risk go away. There is much you can do to increase clients' willingness to trust and risk. Start by being more open about your work and yourself. Encourage new clients to talk with old clients. Discuss other projects you have completed—this shows them you know what you are doing. Learn about and respect their organization. Show them that you appreciate how they think and feel about their workplace. Find out what they have done successfully. Demonstrate your belief in them and the business. Point out how you are trying to help them accomplish their ends. Make their goals your goals—and remind them regularly that you and they are working for the same thing.

When you see risky situations, point them out and help clients deal with them. Be a model risk taker. Show them that you too are willing to risk to serve their ends. Voice your doubts and fears as well as your hopes and aspirations. Demonstrate that you are not fearless, just as they are not. Follow through on all your commitments. Be with clients the way you want them to be with you. If you want more openness, then be open. If you want them to listen, then listen more yourself. Share responsibility for getting work done. Holding it all to yourself encourages the opposite of trusting and risking.

You will learn more about how to build trust and the willingness to risk when you approach clients knowing that your partnership must include both elements in order to work.

Part Three

The Consultant

Nine

Love at Work

ove entered my consulting vocabulary years ago. Though I didn't use the word much, love was there, and it was legitimate. I thought about love at work more often than I talked about it with clients. I chose to see its emerging importance to me as wisdom rather than as a softening of my brain and heart. At this point in my consulting career, love is even more apparent to me; I see it all around me when I am working. But we do not do enough to acknowledge its presence and importance. I mean, what would it sound like if executives told of a love for each other! Shocking!! So we don't talk much about it, we show it a little, and we want to show it more.

We all want love, and our wants do not respect the boundaries of work. Many people show up for the money but stay for love. They assume they will get the money; they seek love. Yet many would deny it. But just watch them during their work day: What are they searching for, what do they respond to? Attention, recognition, care, understanding, affection, glory, respect, appreciation, inclusion . . . they're looking for love in all the *right* places. Yes, we show up at work seeking love in one form or another, and if you were to dissolve those feelings among people, many organizations would fall apart. Certainly, there are other glues that hold organizations together, but love is one.

This chapter is not about "love for sale" in corporate America; this is not about lust and sex—though it might be about passion. This chapter is about needs that make us human and that we don't leave at home when we go to the office. This chapter is about a progression through love of self, love of others, and love of work. What I say is based on my own experience and my observations of others. Like everyone, I often do not love myself, my clients, and my work. But when I do, I am more successful in my consulting life and in the rest of my life too. Consider the simple five-level hierarchy illustrated here, which starts at the bottom with *know* and culminates in the "L" word.

Five Levels of Appreciation

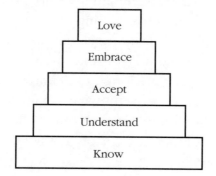

This short hierarchy is even steeper than it looks. These are the levels we need to move through in deepening appreciation. Keep these levels in mind while you read this chapter. I will clarify them as I write about working toward love of ourselves, others, and our work.

Love of Self

Love of self is not necessary to achieve professional success, stature, or recognition—though it can help. You and I don't have to love ourselves or our work to have clients or make money. The world has demonstrated this more times than we have cared to learn from. But if you want enjoyment, abundance, growth, opportunity, and a high yield on life, then love yourself, love others, and love your work.

Loving yourself comes first. Love of self is what opens you to loving others and your work. How many times have I found that what was blocking me with others was something I was having difficulty accepting in myself? I must move through a knowing to an understanding of myself, to an acceptance of what I understand, to an embracing of what I accept, and to a loving of what I embrace. When I have moved through this hierarchy completely, I can love myself. To be realistic, I acknowledge that I am always working at new understandings of who I am and what I mean. I am always struggling to accept some parts of myself. I embrace a lot that I am and distance myself from other parts of me. I love much more of myself than I used to, but still have pieces I don't want to look at, much less love. Much of that work within myself is yet to be done.

Love of Others

Follow through the five levels of appreciation with me as we look at love of others. Notice how these levels fit and do not fit with your thoughts. Let's imagine starting at the bottom of this hierarchy and working to the top to develop a full professional relationship with a client.

1. *Know.* I see a potential client on the horizon. I collect information about that client. I go to the client's website for information; I do a search to find out more about the organization. I gather and review data about the client. I begin to see that other levels of appreciation are possible and that they will be informed by what I learn here. I know the client.

2. *Understand.* I seek the meaning behind the knowledge I've gathered—as the client understands it and as I understand it. I meet with the client; I express some of what I know and ask questions to deepen my understanding. I express what I understand, and the client confirms that I do understand. I know and understand the client—and the client knows this as well.

3. *Accept.* To accept the client requires openness, allowance, welcome; it does not necessarily mean to agree. Rather, it means that I see the client as a person of value, worth my attention. My acceptance is larger than any individual point that might come up between us. I accept the client for who he is, for what he says, what he does, what he feels. I know, understand, and accept the client—and the client knows this.

4. *Embrace.* Embracing a client eliminates the distance between us that still exists at the acceptance level. This is a hard notion to express; it resembles acceptance but is clearly beyond it. A physical embrace is a good symbol for what I do with the client's thoughts and feelings. I enfold the client's ideas, emotions, issues, and opportunities. I wrap my own thoughts and feelings around his; I honor what is important to the client because it is important to him—even when I disagree strongly. At this point, I know, understand, accept, and embrace the client—and the client knows this.

5. *Love.* The top level of appreciation is love of the client. How does love "work" at work? In its ideal expres-

sion, distinctions between the client and myself are less important. We are attuned to each other. We open to each other, without fear of each other. Neither of us needs to change to satisfy the other. We each have complete trust that the other will act in ways that serve us both well. There is no need to be protective in any way. And this love builds on my knowing, understanding, accepting, and embracing the client.

Many of us say we love our work. It seems absurd to me that we should not open ourselves to loving the peo ple with whom we do our work. As in other loving relationships, the ascent of this hierarchy is accompanied by risk, but it can bring new depth to our partnerships with clients. Look for opportunities to care for clients more. Look into the work they are doing and find what deserves respect, admiration, praise, or honor. See their work from a larger life perspective. See it as the way they have chosen to invest themselves, to find meaning in their lives. Find out about what they do outside of work—their hobbies, their families, their community work. All of this will help you build your love for your clients and will help you help them.

Love of Work

It is wonderful to hear someone say, "I love my work!" whether they are clients or fellow consultants. I wish more of us were saying it, and I am convinced that more of us could love our work if we allowed ourselves to. Many people could even love their present work if they could just change their perspective on it. Some have been too busy complaining about work to recognize that they get a great deal out of doing this work each day. Others may have to leave what they are doing and face the uncertainty of moving to a happier but unfamiliar job.

Think about the work you do now and where you are on the hierarchy: Which parts of your work are you just getting to know and understand? Which are you struggling to accept or embrace? Which parts of your work do you love? If you don't love your work and for many months or years have not found elements of it to love, then get out of it. Life is too important and work is too important to life to spend years doing something you do not want to be doing. Extenuating circumstances certainly affect your decision, but try not to use a child's education or a parent's illness as the excuse to continue doing work you can't stand. Aim higher and consider how you would go about getting work that you would love to do. This consideration is not a commitment. After you've decided what you would love to do, you can decide whether you are going to do anything about this decision. Do not block yourself from thinking about it; you will never learn what you do not allow yourself to think about.

The marketplace offers us the opportunity to define the kind of work we would like to do and then go out to find clients who provide what we are seeking. Yes, there are risks that come with this opportunity. I can think of at least nine different directions I have taken in my work as I have sought out what is important to me. I have analyzed business systems, done business research, trained managers, assessed executives, built teams, developed strategies, redesigned work, envisioned futures, and written books all because I was open to what I might love to do. What I am doing now is miles from what I was doing when I started more than thirty years ago. I love the fact that by pursuing a love of work, I have moved through so many different kinds of work.

If this chapter on love and appreciation posed some difficulty for you, perhaps you can take some comfort in knowing that I had trouble writing it. I was tempted to leave the chapter out, but that would have supported the workplace denial of the presence of love. I want you to consider love's consequences for your work. Love can increase your personal power, your meaningfulness, and your effectiveness.

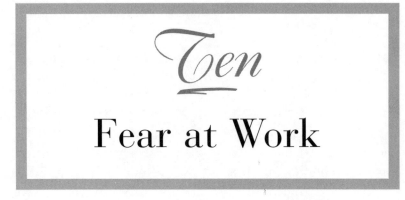

Fear at Work

This chapter is about the fears that come with doing consulting work—our own fears and the fears of our clients, the normal fears that accompany work in organizations. Most of our fears are a natural outgrowth of change. Some deeper fears can arise from real personal trauma. While doing this work, we occasionally make unintended connections; someone becomes deeply afraid because what is being asked of him represents a tragedy from his past. That has happened to me in my work, and it is not the kind of fear I am writing about here.

My youngest daughter used to ask wonderful "what if" questions. "What if we go off the cliff?" "What if the trees fall on our house?" "What if Bigfoot jumps on the roof of our car?" We laughed because we knew how unlikely it was that the disaster she feared would happen. And our laughter was tinged with our own irrational fears. My work has given me a closet full of these what-ifs. Let's open the door a crack and see what scampers out:

What if they have the wrong [e-mail address, website, phone number, street address], so they can't reach me even though they are trying? What if my answering service is not working, so I don't know they are calling? What if nobody is even trying to call?

What if I am missing the point? What if I really don't understand what is going on here? What if somebody asks me a question at the meeting, and I don't know the answer? What if I break down and cry?!

What if my insightful comment is just drivel? What if I am not as smart as I think I am? What if I have just been lucky and fooling people, and they are discovering the truth about me?

What if I screw this up? What if, as a result of my efforts, everything ends up being worse than it was before they asked for my help? What if lots of people are hurt in the process? . . . and they fire me? And then they tell everybody about how bad I was! And they sue me! And my name is in the newspaper! And I am disgraced!

Upon seeing my list, other consultants might have some additions. What if . . .

I don't get it right?	I have bad breath?
It isn't perfect?	I'm dressed wrong?
They are giving me bad data?	My fly is open?
I'm late?	Their check bounces?
My check bounces?	They don't like me?

Yes, there is a lot to worry about—if we choose to worry. Our own what-if questions provide clues to our deeper fears, and patterns of what-ifs are bigger clues. What-ifs anticipate disastrous answers, answers that have what-ifs of their own that yield even worse consequences. What-ifs are rich ground from which to dig out our fears.

Notice where you dig, where you return to dig, again and again. What are the embarrassments, losses, humiliations, and pains that you regularly anticipate, even when they do not occur as regularly as you expect them? Have you ever said something like, "That would be so embarrassing—I'd just die!" Now *that* is a disastrous consequence! Fears are rooted in our past and have no necessary connection to this moment unless we create it. In that sense they are irrational, yet they are real and do influence our behavior.

My clients also have fears. I can work better with theirs when I acknowledge my own. When I am working with clients on their fears, I risk being more open with my own. One of my most common ways of connecting with clients is related to our shared fears. When I see them doing something that I interpret as related to their fears, I begin searching for similar fears in myself. Then I speak from the place of someone who has known fear and faced it. Wondering, doubting, questioning, worrying, and fearing are part of the process of making changes in our work and lives. Sitting around talking about our fears does not move us forward, but it is still progress; it clears the path ahead so that the "real work" can begin.

Tips on Dealing with Fear

It helps to acknowledge fear as normal—despite the fact that few people around you are acknowledging it. Do not believe only what you see and hear in most business meetings or at monthly professional meetings; this does not represent the whole truth. The people there share your doubts, and if you could ever begin talking together about these doubts, you would have a much more meaningful discussion than most folks are having at the meeting.

Expressing your fears aloud to the right people helps relieve everyone's fears.

Respect the fears that people carry. This is not an easy burden. Whether rooted in a clear and present danger or in a distant memory, fear is real and deserves respect. When you do not respect the fear others carry, they will withhold themselves from you, you will not know them, and you will be less effective in dealing with them.

Help yourself and others laugh at fears. Fears may be serious, but there is more than one way of looking at them. Laughing does not eliminate fears, but laughter does give us some power over them by taking us outside them. Seen from the outside, fears look different than they do when we are caught inside them. Help people laugh at themselves by laughing at yourself. You, the person who repeatedly fears that the world is coming to an end—and then it doesn't. You, the person who worries that nobody likes him—and is telling a close friend about this. I am sure that much of what you do with your fears is *very* funny when seen from the outside. Laughter can be part of keeping our anxieties in perspective. We do not eliminate them, but we do see the larger world around them, which can cause their power to fade.

Failure

A few years ago, a project with a favorite long-term client organization came apart. I was leading a three-day meeting and stopped it midway because it was not working. And I knew whose fault it was: not mine! I flew back to the safety of my office, put the box of meeting materials in the corner, and blamed the people I'd worked with, especially one of them, for the failure.

That sealed box sat there for over a year. Each time I looked at it, I was reminded of the failed project and the people who let me down. I tried to open the box to file away its contents, but I couldn't; something wouldn't let me. The box sat there. And gnawed at me. One day, in a moment of insight, I confronted myself: What had I done to contribute to the failure of the project? For over a year I had not asked that question. When I finally thought about it, I could see that I had been more than a contributor: I had been the major cause! What a shock! I felt horrible!

Over a year too late, I made telephone calls and wrote notes to the primary person with whom I had worked. My calls and notes got no response, though I know they were received. I expressed my shame and my apologies. And I was finally able to open the box and put its contents away. Discovering the hard truth brought both pain and relief.

What do you do with failure? What are your inclinations, actions, and feelings? You saw mine in the story I just told. What stories could you tell? We are people; we will succeed, and we will fail. Do not doubt any of that. But what do we *do* with failure?

When a project comes apart or is taken apart, feel bad about it. Indulge yourself; make time to wallow in the bad feelings. You cannot go around them; you must go through them. Do not become prematurely rational. Instead, discover what you deeply feel when your work does not work. When you recover too quickly, you don't get to understand what is going on inside you. You must step into feeling bad to discover whether you feel disappointed, angry, misunderstood, hurt, embarrassed, ashamed, or insignificant. Experiencing your feelings rather than burying them brings more of a catharsis. Your intense reactions often have more to do with your personal history than with the failure that provoked the reaction. When your reactions are more intense and lasting than the current situation can explain, something else is at work, perhaps a trauma or difficulty from earlier in your life.

Learn. Notice the source and intensity of your feelings: Have you had these kinds of feelings before? Is there a familiar pattern to these feelings? If you see a pattern, can you stand back and notice the phases you commonly undergo in processing these feelings? When you have particularly intense emotional reactions, take a look into your early life: What happened then that might support these intense feelings you are having now as an adult? You don't need therapy; just learn what you can from this experience of failure so that you will be more ready for the next one. I'm sorry, but yes, this is going to happen again! And remember that the ways you deal with your own failures, big and small, affect how you deal with your clients when failure looms.

Eleven

Searching Your Shadows

$\mathcal{W}$e do not know as much about ourselves as we think. We act as if "what you see is what you get." That's only half the truth: what you *don't* see is what you get too! This chapter is about those parts, sides, and corners of ourselves that we do not know well, those sides not often exposed to the light of day. Because they are part of us and hidden from us, they represent an opportunity for self-discovery. What is hidden from us may be good, bad, threatening, liberating, wonderful, awful; we do not know. What I have learned is that whatever is there has power, and that power is increased through being hidden. That hidden power may be new life options waiting to be released. Whenever we discover more about who we are, we are empowered. You are who you are whether you know it or not. Knowing more about yourself opens your alternatives and possibilities. This chapter shines a little light into our darker corners—just a little light.

This discussion is part of our personal work in becoming more complete individuals and consultants, and it is part of how we discover and "enlighten" our clients. Shadow and darkness have everything to do with consulting. Part of consulting has to do with finding our clients' hidden corners, their power, their acceptance, and their alternatives. When we shine a little light into their dark corners, we help them discover what they already are—whether they knew it or not. If we have done this for ourselves first, we are better able to hold the light for them.

Looking into Our Dark Corners

How would you look into these dark corners? Whether for your clients or yourself, that is a tough question to answer. Just writing about the subject makes me nervous. My own shadows are hanging over my shoulder looking at what I type, seeing how honest and useful I will be. I will offer five suggestions that have helped me discover more about myself and my clients. Then I will guide you on an exploration of your own. First, the suggestions:

Move toward your discomfort. Search out a part of yourself that has shown a pattern of making you uncomfortable in your life and your work. Agree with yourself that you are going to move toward it, look at it, seek to understand it, shine some light on it. Remind yourself that this is your choice; you do not have to do this. You can move ahead or quit, as you like.

Name it. Put a label on this shadowy, less known part of yourself. In doing that, you legitimize it; you make it a "thing"; you give it identity and boundaries. In an

Alcoholics Anonymous meeting, you can hear person after person declare, "My name is _____, and I am an alcoholic." In a similar way, you can declare, "I am an angry person!" or "I am afraid of failing," or "I can't handle success." Whatever it might be, make a declaration about yourself that identifies something you usually avoid thinking about.

Acknowledging a weak or secret part of myself can be a step toward resolution. First I need to acknowledge it to myself, and then I may be ready to acknowledge it to others. Acknowledging it to myself is difficult because I have to step into the reality of the weakness or secret more than I have in the past. I have fearfully avoided it. I'd rather not think about it, thank you very much! I fear that if I look at it, it will be awful, and I will be consumed, swallowed by the beast in me. Well, that's not what has happened, at least for me . . . so far.

Experience it. Whether "it" is anger, achievement, sadness, joy, depression, love—whatever it is, find a way of experiencing it more deeply than you have allowed yourself in the past. Find a safe way of expressing this less known self, a way that goes beyond what you usually do and helps you learn more about it. Discover more about that dark corner by moving toward it, into it, and feeling what it is like to be there.

Read about it. Chances are there are a dozen books written by and about people much like you. Learn from them; enjoy the support they provide through their books. Look online for information and discussions about the shadowy area that concerns you. Follow other people's thinking, feelings, and guidance. There is no reason to explore this alone.

Talk about it. Acknowledge that part of yourself to others. Not to everyone at once, but try it out on someone important to you. "I have been exploring the part of myself that is very, very angry." Or find a group of friends willing to engage in serious discussion; talk with them about your shadowy explorations.

Moving beyond self-awareness to let others in on my secrets brings a different kind of threat and opportunity. When I reveal something I have not shown others in the past, there is the possibility of complete rejection! There is also the possibility of total acceptance, and this could make it worth trying. If I gain the acceptance I dare to hope for, I can be more myself with these people from this point forward. I don't have to pretend any longer. A burden is lifted, and I can make better use of those energies I had been using to protect myself.

These five suggestions let you reveal yourself to you and others. Following them would increase the light and reduce the shadows in your corners. Our initial, reactive fear is about what is hidden in shadow that we do not know. Bringing hidden parts of ourselves out into the light reduces that fear and releases the power held by the hidden unknown.

Once I have acknowledged my shadowy side to myself and others, I don't have to behave in the same old ways anymore—at least with the people I have involved. I can go on to something better for me. I can behave in new ways—that may or may not work. New fears confront me: the fear of behaving in new ways, and related fears about how well the new ways will work. What if I do it wrong? What if it doesn't work? What if I screw it up? And here we go again. Another learning and growing opportunity.

This chapter promotes looking into the shadows as a path to personal growth. Frankly, there is nothing more important to me as a consultant than becoming myself more fully, and I am suggesting that this might be just as important to you. You can load yourself down with all your consulting models and tools and methods and techniques, but they do not operate themselves. They are all used by you with your clients, who are looking for your uniqueness. They will see whether you are a skilled consultant using your talents with integrity, or merely a mechanic carrying a tool box.

Searching the Shadows: An Exploration

If you are intrigued by this chapter, work through this exploration—shine light into some of your dark corners—to discover a little more about yourself. Don't worry about your response; just work through the process for as many steps as you find useful. You need one sheet of paper, a pen, and twenty minutes.

1. Relax for a moment and step back from your work. Think about what you have been doing over the last year, who you have worked with, what has gone well, what didn't work so well, what was on your mind, how you felt during this time.

2. In thinking about yourself in your work, consider your concerns. What makes you uncomfortable? What worries you, makes you anxious, or upsets you? What makes you uncomfortable? This is likely something you return to, again and again, the kind of thing you think about at three in the morning; it keeps you awake. You may even see a pattern of pursuing this same worry over years. And you do not want other people to know about it, especially your clients. You might tell a close friend about this,

but you wouldn't want other people to know about it. It's a secret, and you go out of your way to avoid acknowledging it.

3. In a few lines or a short paragraph, describe to yourself what it is you repeatedly worry about and do not want others, especially your clients, to know about.

4. Next, consider what you do to keep clients from knowing about this worry of yours. What do you do to hide it? How do you keep your secret? How do you pretend? Write a short list of things you have done to protect yourself and your secret.

5. Why is this secret so important to you? What are you protecting by taking the actions you take? Think for a few minutes about what the secret represents, and write about it. Look back earlier in your life to see whether anything there explains the importance of the secret now.

6. Consider how much energy you put into this worry, this anxiety, this secret. Consider the time you spend on it, the ways you protect yourself and what that involves, the stories you tell, the energy you invest. Write a line or two attempting to quantify or make tangible how much energy you put into this anxiety.

7. To this point, you have described a worry you do not want clients to know about. You have considered what you do to keep them from knowing; you have explored why it is so important to keep this secret; you have estimated how much energy all of this takes. And all of that is written on one page. You have pulled all your thoughts together in one place; you are a little clearer about the game you play, and how and why you play it.

8. Fold up the paper and put it in a place where you can find it each day. Read the page twice a day—each morning and each evening—for at least five work days.

9. During these five days and nights, notice yourself doing what you wrote about on the paper. Do not change anything in your behavior; do what you usually do and notice the effects on you and the people around you. Notice the energy it takes; notice the consequences of your behavior; notice how much you do to keep your secret.

Sometimes when we give our secrets more attention, we become aware of what a burden they are. That's a first step toward doing something more about them. You may or may not want to do something about your secret after five days; my goal for this exploration is to increase your awareness of what you are choosing to do and the impact of those choices. That's all.

Here is what one person wrote in going through the nine steps:

> *I often worry about my competence; I am afraid my clients will discover that I am not as experienced a consultant as I act like I am. As a result of this anxiety, I go into meetings overprepared; I spend far too much time on my work, taking that time away from my family, and that irritates them. And I find myself exaggerating my accomplishments with my clients, making me look better than I really am. I lie awake at night thinking through what I did that day, or will do the next day. Frequently I get up and make notes. Whenever a client calls, my reaction is, "What went wrong? Do they still want me? Have they found me out?" This is such a big anxiety for me; it consumes lots of energy that could be used in much better ways. I've always been like this, even back in school as a kid, I was concerned that I was not good enough.*

Imagine this person reading her paragraph twice each day and reminding herself of her secret. She might see the effect of her secret more clearly. She might even want to act on her new awareness. If she chose to act, I'd suggest that she share what she has written and felt over the five days—with someone she trusts. It's one thing to understand your game; it's quite another to reveal it to others, thereby changing it.

All of this applies to our work with organizations; they have shadows and games too. In their way, they too go through these struggles for identity, clarity, and authenticity. They deceive and are unwilling to come to terms with their behavior. We can help them do something like the exploratory exercise I've described—not blaming, but noticing the effects and burdens that come with presenting a false self. We can legitimize an organization's talking about things that are not working well. We can help clients acknowledge their secrets and games and help them move on. No one is served by pretending that this organization is noble, clear, enlightened, and perfect. Move a few secrets out of the shadows and see what happens. The shadow side and the light side need each other, in our lives and in the lives of organizations with which we work.

This chapter is more personal than many other chapters in this book. It applies directly to our work as consultants, but is more about our lives as individuals. If we are going to bring who we are to what we do, we need to bring our entire selves—not just the parts we like and are willing to show in public. We can strengthen ourselves by becoming better acquainted with those parts of ourselves we have left hidden in the shadows. We will be better consultants to the extent that we are better, more complete individuals. Our clients will notice; they will be drawn to our authenticity and power, and we will help them see their own.

The Consultant
as Leader

*I*n my early years as a consultant, I saw myself as a kind of organizational lubricant. I was an enabler, a helper working with clients to free up rusty parts, a kind of human WD-40 that allowed the organizational gears to turn more quickly and quietly. Those were the days when I was taken with the dynamics among individuals in a group. In meetings, you would hear me make comments like, "John, I am noticing that as you talk, you maintain eye contact with Phil and seldom look at others in the group," or "Gertrude, if you were to rephrase your question and make it a statement, what would it be?" or "It sounds like the team is about to make a decision. I have noticed that most of you have not spoken during the discussion." My observations were usually new information for these groups, and it often enriched their conversations and improved their effectiveness. I facilitated what they were doing—a useful role that I enjoyed playing. But it was not enough for me. Something was missing.

As helpful as it was to keep the wheels turning, I didn't get to say where the wheels ought to go. There was no room to ask questions about whether the wheels ought to turn at all, or whether these were the particular wheels that ought to turn. When questions like these came up in meetings, I was silent. These considerations were outside the way I had learned and defined my role. I knew I had more to contribute. I confirmed this with others. I spoke with clients about what I wanted to do and gained their support. I began to stretch the boundaries of my facilitator role. I began to offer ideas on the content discussed in meetings. I made room for others to pick up the facilitator role, relying less on me. In the heat of discussion, I would question strategies, offer new ideas about direction, or offer alternatives. In other words, I began to put forth all the ideas I had bottled up in the past. And this went very well for my clients; they generally liked what they were getting. My excitement for my work increased. Clients began to ask me to lead rather than to sit in on meetings.

I began to see myself as an organizational leader bringing my own special talents and responsibilities—just like everyone else in the room. Of course I do not forget that I am a consultant; my commitment is different and less. I know that I cannot make decisions, but I can advise strongly. I know that I do not carry the responsibilities that come with being an executive or a worker who shows up every day. But I now know that I am not here just to help clients with their agenda. I have my own agenda and pursue it openly. I respect the clients' agenda and will yield to it; it is their organization, not mine. I have less knowledge about the intricacies of their business and make a point of showing my respect for the knowledge and experience they bring.

When I believe I understand their issues and have a strong opinion, I offer it. Silence on issues does not serve them or me well. I am willing to lead major parts of meetings, to design a structure and work through it to outcomes they support. I am willing to offer alternatives to clients that go beyond what they have developed. When I see possible action, I recommend it. I think and act as if I were a part of this organization—knowing that I am not. I push, pull, argue, pontificate, praise, joke, and join with them as we produce together. And much of the time, I am silent and supportive like other group members. Though it is legitimate for me to be at the center of issues, I do not have to be there.

No, I do not tell clients how to make steel, educate kids, design chips, hatch salmon, or make candy. I participate less in those technical core functions, except to ask questions and understand. The content I do wade into is usually related to the changes they are trying to bring about. You might hear me say such things as "I've listened to all of you, and I think you ought to . . .," or "It sounds like this committee wants to . . .," or even "I think you are about to make a bad decision. It's your organization, but this decision would hurt you." Combining my old facilitator role with the leader role looks something like this: "What have we been doing for the last thirty minutes? I don't think you are ready to make this decision," or "I think that Herb is making a good point and that the rest of you are not hearing what he is saying."

None of this assumes that I am the only leader; I follow others' lead most of the time. When a meeting is going well, I can watch the leadership move from person to person as the subject and each person's investment or responsibility require. As a client said to his executive committee once, "I don't know exactly what Geoff does, but I do know that we have better meetings and make better decisions when he is around." That is the kind of comment I treasure. Another executive once said to me, "I want to remind you that I am the president and I will decide." He saw me overstepping my bounds and called me on it. He was right. Yes, there are potential problems in stepping out of the observer-commentator role and onto the playing field. The power dynamics shift, and I put more at risk.

You may want to move toward leadership if you hold strong beliefs and values about your work. If you find yourself frequently holding back your opinions and in doing so depriving your clients of something they could use, get support from your clients to speak up more. Talk with them about your current role and how you would like to supplement it. Do not experiment too much without getting their agreement, however. Remember to keep their best interests at heart. This is not just about you and your opinions; this is about them and about serving their larger purposes.

Thirteen

Building Your Power

ower is variously defined as the ability to choose, to act, and to influence or control others. Or to cause others to act, to get what you want. My favorite definition is this: *power is knowing what you want and acting on it.* The accent on self-knowledge is essential to powerful action. Power comes with joined responsibilities: knowing and doing. It contains the potential for abuse, for being self-centered, but it also can be used in service to others. Power is both a potentially positive and a potentially negative force. It is available to everyone and essential for life.

Power has developed negative connotations over the years because we have seen it abused. But it is the abuse we need to eliminate, not the power itself. These abuses cause me to hesitate to say that I want power. We often equate a person's seeking power with an excessive need to control, selfishness, and autocracy. These are certainly potential problems, and we will explore that darker side of power in the next chapter. This chapter focuses on

power as essential, positive, and available to everyone—
and important to us in our relationships with clients. We
consultants must be powerful if we are to make a difference. This chapter offers alternative ways of knowing what
you want and acting on it.

Sources of Consulting Power

Power comes in a variety of hues, textures, and sizes that
go far beyond "good" and "bad." Considering alternative
forms of power helps us understand both what our power
is and how we might express it. The power people exercise within organizations can be categorized into one or
more of six types. As you read through the descriptions of
these six kinds of power, think about which descriptions
fit you—or could fit you.

1. *Power of authority.* You are a powerful person
because the organization has given you a position of
responsibility. You make decisions that others are expected
to follow. Your position has been formally defined; it is
more permanent than temporary.

2. *Power of association.* Over the years, you have
built a network of solid connections with people in high
places. You know many influential people who are important to the work at hand and will listen to you. You assid-
uously maintain your contacts and let others know that you
do. People pay more attention to you because of your
close connections with these other powerful people.

3. *Power of reward.* You have favors (money, gifts,
smiles, goodies, help, recognition) you can bestow on people when you like what they do. People want these rewards
and will perform differently in order to gain your favors.

4. *Power of punishment.* You can cause minor or major pain for people and not worry about whether they will get back at you. You exercise this power through strong disapproval or withholding your affection or talking about them or depriving them of something they want. You can hurt others emotionally, perhaps even physically, and they know it. They behave differently in order to avoid running afoul of you.

5. *Power of expertise.* Through years of study and application, you have accumulated a wealth of knowledge and talent that others value. People are drawn to you because of this. They want to use your talent or be associated with it.

6. *Power of relationship.* You develop close connections with a variety of people. Many people like you, and you like them. They have a caring or affection for you that you can build on, and vice versa. You have "a place in your heart" for them, and that creates trust and openness.

Which of these six powers do we consultants use? All of them. Sometimes proudly, sometimes secretly, and most of the time, one hopes, with some awareness. And which powers serve us best? We should cultivate the powers of expertise and relationship and be cautious about regularly relying on any of the other four. Let's consider the consequences of using each of these six powers.

Authority. We seldom have this legitimate and permanent power. It comes with being in an organizational position defined and respected as powerful. Any authority and position power we can muster is temporary; our position does not command the same respect or attention that others in authority have. We cannot count on having this power, so we cannot build our power base on it. As is true of the other powers, this does not mean we never use authority power; it just means that we cannot rely on it over time.

Association. We often associate with organizationally powerful people of all kinds. If our associates have any of the six powers and we are close to them, we are identified as having some of their power at our disposal. But we have to use this power very carefully. Our powers are less than and circumscribed by theirs. For example, if we are associated with a person who relies on punishment for power, people will see us as being able to bring that punishment down upon them. If our associate relies on authority, we will be looked at as being able to draw on that authority. Although these powers of association are real for us, our power is dependent on that of others. We are better off building power that comes directly from us.

Reward. We do have rewards we can give others. We can recognize contributors to a project; we can reward people with time or attention or public recognition. Whatever we do, some of our actions will be interpreted as reward power. If you hold out a reward for someone in order that she does something you want, you may inadvertently encourage her to seek the reward as her objective, and your real goals become incidental. For example, when a parent offers a child a quarter to take out the trash, the child may try taking out the trash four times a day—not what the parent intended! We consultants do use reward power, but not as a primary source.

Punishment. We all have this power, and consultants should avoid using it. Our information about organizations and their members is privileged. So is our position. When we use that information or our position to punish people, we jeopardize our standing. Our success relies on gathering accurate information and establishing open, trusting relationships with people. Punishment runs counter to what we are about. Granted, some of our actions will be seen as punishing, because our work affects people's jobs. We can agree with people about how we will use what we learn, and how we will deal with them can reduce the risks related to punishment power. In a sense, we can intentionally disempower ourselves with regard to our privileged information. Even apart from the fact that it hurts others, punishment power is not a reliable way for us to get things done. Using it encourages others to fall back on that power too; they want to get us back.

Expertise. Expertise is our initial, presenting power. Expertise gets us in the door, justifies our presence, and causes people to listen to us. We are highly reliant on this power; without it, we aren't here. It is earned moment to moment, in contrast to authority, which relies on position rather than performance. We can establish lasting expert power by acquiring and exercising skills, experience, perspective, knowledge, or wisdom that supplement what the client already possesses. This is one essential power for consultants, but it seldom stands alone.

Relationship. This is the second essential consultant power. As I've mentioned elsewhere, our work requires the client to take risks, risk taking requires trust, and trust requires relationship power. Expert power can be built up and stored, but relationship power must be husbanded; it is quite perishable. Without it, we will not be doing the work we want to do, the work we are capable of doing. With it, we have the potential for long-term work.

Expertise and relationship combine to provide the foundation for effective, lasting partnerships. Cultivate both. Do not neglect the powers of authority, association, reward, and punishment—you will be wielding them whether you know it or not—but do not regularly rely on them to build your practice.

Power Comes Through Perception

The six powers we've been discussing are not absolute; they exist to the extent that people recognize their presence. If people do not perceive them, these powers flag or fail. Power is a dynamic among people and is mostly a function of perception. Power is like a common currency that you pass among yourselves.

Although we could talk about any of the six powers, let's use the power of expertise to look at how perception affects power. If you have expertise but do not recognize it, you use it less. Your power with others is diminished because you will not be using it as frequently or as well. If you have expertise but your clients do not know it, they can't turn to you for guidance. Your power is diminished by what they do not know. If neither you nor they recognize the power of your expertise, you might as well not have the expertise.

When you perceive that you have expertise, your power is increased; you will initiate, involve yourself, and see yourself as a legitimate participant. When your expertise is not perceived by others but is only a self-perception, you will be seen as less effective—even if initially you act in more powerful ways because of your belief in yourself. When others perceive that you have expertise and they value expertise, your power with them is increased—whether you in fact have expertise or not. Conversely, when others perceive that you do not have the expertise they value, your power is decreased with them—no matter how smart you may be on the subject. The currency of power initially moves in the direction of perceived power—regardless of whether real power is there.

This combination of reality and perception gets very complicated for everyone, but especially for us in our client-consultant relationships. Even if we confine ourselves to the power of expertise, there are many possible permutations between us and our client. Add more clients, and the possible variations start expanding. Add the five other powers, and the complications increase geometrically.

Managing Our Powers

These powers are the source of our strength. People, including our clients, are drawn to our strength. Our potential for power with clients is strong; the question is how we will use our power.

Imagine yourself as an international banker with six different currencies stacked in front of you. You possess more of some currencies than others; some of the currencies are stronger in the market, more respected than others. You are trying to profit from the use of these six currencies. Your supply of currencies is considerable and reliable, but not inexhaustible. In the face of the market, how will you use the currencies available to you? In what combination? With what intensity? For how long? In which directions? We consultants are like this banker: we must build our currencies—our powers—and maintain them by using them well.

Clients have ways and reasons for putting consultants up on power pedestals, and we consultants sometimes silently participate in the conspiracy to elevate ourselves. As we increase our power, we must be careful not to reduce that of our clients. When they want us to have the answers to their questions and the solutions to their problems, we can take too much responsibility for providing all the right answers and finding all the best solutions. As we increase our power by feeding their dependence on us, we help weaken them. Centuries ago, Confucius spoke of the importance of teaching people how to fish, rather than feeding them a fish a day. If he were speaking to consultants today, he might say, "Quit fishing for your clients! Quit feeding your clients a fish a day! Teach them to fish. Teach them to design fishing nets and fishing boats. Teach them to market and sell fish. Teach them to build fish distribution networks." Well, Confucius might not say all that, but you get my point.

Although I see consultants primarily as guides who help clients use their own resources better, we sometimes have useful answers and solutions. That truth complicates our exercise of power. It would be much cleaner if we were always in a helping role, but we are not—at least, I am not. Our experience reinforces our opinions. Hours of work in a system shape our biases about what ought to be done. Listening to the client work out alternatives stimulates alternatives in our own minds. When we bring our opinions, biases, and alternatives forward, we step out of the background into the foreground, and our role has changed. So has our exercise of our power.

Our power dilemmas come because we are powerful; we know what we want and want to act on it. And we are doing this in someone else's organization. We need to be very conscious of our client, our role, and our powers. When we discuss role with our clients, we are also discussing the kind and degree of power we will be exercising.

In early meetings with clients, propose what your role might be; test it on them. Ask them for their ideas; see what they think. For example, if you were leading a planning session, would it be appropriate for you to step beyond your role as meeting leader to offer your opinions on the subject being discussed? Are all your contributions welcome? When you are in the middle of consulting—carrying out your role—you can remind people of what you are doing, why you are doing it, and how this fits with the agreements on what your role is in this situation. You remind them because they may have forgotten your role, and you want them to know that you have not forgotten. While you are working, keep in mind the role (and power) agreements you have. Clients are more comfortable discussing role than power, but the dynamics around execution of role are power dynamics.

Finding Your Power: An Exploration

This exercise can help you pull together the thoughts you have been accumulating while reading this chapter. Take thirty minutes to work through the first three steps, then try applying what you have learned there to steps four through seven.

1. What powers do you have as an individual and as a consultant? Write a paragraph about yourself that puts your powers in the context of your life and work. Review the six powers described earlier, apply them to yourself, and write about them.

2. List the powers you think others—especially clients—attribute to you. Do not dwell on whether you agree or disagree with those perceptions; just list them.

3. Compare the client powers list to your own list. Notice where you have real or perceived powers that your clients do not perceive or value. And notice the powers they assign to you that you did not put on your personal list.

4. Use the paragraph you wrote in step one to adjust what you say about yourself to clients. Be alert for ways to give appropriate expression to your power. This helps others see you as powerful.

5. Find out more about the ways in which clients see you as powerful. Ask them. Have a heart-to-heart talk with a client with whom you work especially well. When clients hire you, ask why they hired you. When a project is going particularly well, ask the clients about the specific ways you are helping. Ask a power-related question, be quiet, listen to the answer, and appreciate it. Try to stay out of the way so that you hear clients' perceptions rather than your projections.

6. Talk with your friends about what makes you powerful in their lives. If your personal and professional lives are congruent, then many of the powers that your friends attribute to you can be transferred to your work as a consultant.

7. Ask friends how they think you might be fooling yourself in your approach to your life and your work. For example, some of us diminish ourselves by holding self-perceptions that are less powerful than we really are. Others of us elevate ourselves inappropriately by holding a self-perception that is grander than the reality. What do your friends say to you about this?

As we discussed in this chapter, much of power is rooted in perception. As a consultant, you need to know about the real powers you rely on and bring to your work as well as the powers you are perceived to have. You can start sorting out your powerful self-perceptions. Then you can move on to seeing how others see you. By increasing your awareness of both your real and perceived power, you increase your effectiveness with clients.

Misusing Your Power

This book would be less than honest if we talked only about the positive powers we can gain as consultants. There is a darker side to all of this—not just because we are consultants, but because we are people with complex motives for what we do. Our reasons for being in this work are not all in service to higher world purposes and our clients' betterment. No, we are in service to ourselves and the sometimes small worlds we are building around ourselves. Our investments in changing the world or fooling ourselves frequently play out in destructive ways. Denying this blinds us to what we are doing with our clients and, more important, what we are doing with ourselves in our lives.

This chapter dwells on the shadowy side of our work. Unfortunately, it also gives you glimpses of that side of me. Read this not as a confession but as an acknowledgment and acceptance of a part of reality from which many of us turn away. The chapter categorizes common human abuses that apply to consulting; think about how they apply to you. I want myself—and maybe you—to be more honest about the work we do, why we do it, and how we do it. Part of dealing with this shadowy self is bringing it out into the light.

How might the temptations of power and recognition, the avoidance of truth and imperfection, affect what we consultants do with our clients? How might our unacknowledged personal needs show up in our work? Look through this sample laundry list; see whether there is anything here that you would privately acknowledge as something you have done—or have been tempted to do.

- The consultant violates the terms under which the information was gathered by sharing information in a way that the providers did not support at the time they gave the information.
- The consultant uses his expert power to sell an alternative to the client—an alternative from which the consultant will benefit—without including other alternatives.
- The consultant accentuates and distorts the data gathered so as to make the problems of the organization more evident—because the consultant knows better than the data.
- The consultant behaves as if she understands more about a client's situation than she actually does.
- The consultant acts as if he has more expertise than he actually has, leading the client to consult on matters that the consultant in truth knows little about.

We consultants have many ways of misusing our power for the purpose of elevating our image. And why might we do such things? What could be so important that we would be willing to distort, pretend, manipulate, or deceive? Perhaps we are seeking the power we never had in our personal lives. Or we might be trying to live up to an image we think we have created in others' minds. Maybe we are willing to twist things a little if that helps to right the organization's wrongs. Or perhaps we think our manipulation serves some higher purpose. Or maybe we just know better than others.

Ego, vanity, expertise, control, recognition, aspirations, fear, anxiety—all reasons why we consultants choose to abuse the powers given us. Many of us privately redraw the lines of fairness in order to serve what we think the organization needs. Because we presume to help organizations bring about change, we have a responsibility to think about the ways we dispense our influence. We need to think about how far can we push our clients and whether we are imposing our values on them. As we push the limits of our power, we sometimes overreach, serving ourselves before the organization.

The rest of this chapter elaborates on four patterns of abuse of consultant power. I am not talking about an occasional violation of boundaries—we all make mistakes—but of repeated patterns of behavior. As you read about these patterns of superiority, manipulation, pretense, and deception, consider whether they apply to you and whether you have any of your own. We do not want others to know about this kind of behavior when we engage in it; we live in fear that they will find out. Being honest with ourselves begins to break the pattern.

Superiority

Dealing in organizational issues day after day can gradually distort your perspective on what you really know. Being an external consultant has the advantage of distance and encourages feelings of superiority. You can find yourself shifting from "knowing a more effective way" to "knowing the better way" to "I know the best way!" with a hint of "and I am better than you for knowing it." Further, "You are less than I for creating the problems you are caught in." A pattern of this kind of thinking spells trouble for you with your clients—and especially with yourself. Your clients' expectations of you reinforce that part of you that wants to get it right . . . to believe that you really do know what to do all the time . . . that you are an exceptional person . . . with very special talents . . . whom everybody would like to emulate . . . who can do no wrong. . . . Let's face it, you are close to perfect. . . . So of course others should respect your superior wisdom and insight . . . and love you for it! None of this may apply to you, but it does fit some *other* readers of this book.

Consulting feeds those of us inclined to create godlike fantasies about ourselves. Yes, I am occasionally so inclined. The clients invite me in to help, and I do—wonderful! The clients tell me how helpful I am—also wonderful! The clients' actions imply that my kind of talents are what they need around this place full-time—OK. The clients think that I could do a better job with their situation than they could—not so OK. I think I could handle their jobs better than they do—decidedly not OK! That fantasy leads me in the direction of believing in my superiority to them. I create these superior images of myself, I recognize that I do it, and I don't like it.

The reality is that if I were in the middle of the mess they are in, I would be contributing to the mess along with them. I would have helped create it, and I would be stuck in it. In fact, I have similar messes in my own life, outside my work with them. I am able to be of service because I am not part of their organization but an invited and helpful guest with special privileges many of my clients do not get.

From the start, I get people's attention; I get to ask dumb questions, and they are answered; and I get listened to when I speak. I can state my opinions freely; I worry less about impact on my career; I can finish my work and leave. Many clients do not feel they have these special privileges—and I am able to make many of my contributions because I have special access, not because I am special. That's an important distinction to keep in mind when I am feeling superior.

Significant powers do come with our consulting role. We individuals are obviously not irrelevant, but much of the power we have with our clients does not originate with us as individuals. Maintaining our role power depends on our skills, but the power initially comes with the role. I say this not to diminish our importance but to put it in perspective.

Consider the organizations you have belonged to for a long time—as a member, not as a consultant. Perhaps it's the Little League, a church, a long-standing friendship, a reading group, or your family. Think about how you participate in the issues that these organizations have to contend with. When there are problems in Little League, do you behave in the same way you do when you are consulting? Do the other members of your reading group treat you the same way that your clients treat you? Are you accorded the same respect? Does your obvious wisdom and insight carry the day? Does your family care about the fact that you are considered something of an expert in helping organizations work effectively?

My answer to each of these questions is no. I get as trapped in my problems as my clients are trapped theirs. As a member of a group, I struggle to pull myself through the mire. I am more aware of the mire and my stuckness because I am a consultant. In the middle of the muck I am thinking, "I help others resolve problems like this. Why can't I help when it's my problem?" My experience and credentials don't help all that much. For example, my children are not at all impressed with me when we are trying to solve a family problem. In a family meeting years ago, the family told me, "Dad, put away your flip chart!" No, I didn't actually have a chart at the meeting, but I was acting as though I did, and they did not like it.

Reminding myself that I get stuck in much the same way as my clients do is sobering and useful to me. First, it brings me back to reality and returns me to balance by knocking me off my superior perch. Second, I know the experience of being stuck; that makes me a more useful consultant. I empathize with my clients; I know my version of their struggles, and they know that I know. Third, clients sense that I am not blaming them for being stuck, that I accept them in their present condition—because it happens to me and I accept me. Fourth, it emphasizes the obvious: I am human too. I may need that reminder more than my clients do, but it does help them talk directly to me about their foibles, rather than hiding because they think I will be disapproving. In the bigger picture, we are much more like our clients than we are different from them. We are the client too.

Manipulation

If you were being manipulative, you would be pursuing a purpose without being willing to reveal your purpose, intentionally concealing the link between your hidden purpose and your public actions. Others would think you are doing something different from what you really are doing. And you would not want to be found out. You usually know when you are being manipulative, hiding motives because you anticipate negative consequences.

Having done some manipulating, and having been tempted to do much more, I have experienced its risks and consequences. We consultants have unique access to information in our client organizations. Along with that, we often have the ears of the top members of the organization. If we want time with them, our chances of getting it are better than those of most people who work there. And we often have the eyes of the organization on us. That attention puts us in a good position to influence what is going on. Our visibility, our influence, our access—all are made possible by a trust bestowed on us. Everyone expects, or at least hopes, that we will use what we learn in an aboveboard fashion.

That is always my intention, but I have not always honored that intention. Organizations are complex places in which to work, and I am a complex person with needs of my own. During the life of a project, it is not unusual for someone to question whether I am open, whether I can be trusted, whether I am honoring my commitments. These concerns come along with people's discomfort with the risks involved in bringing about change. And sometimes I heighten the concerns through my mistakes; I have misused the trust bestowed on me. While trying to help everyone, I have played both ends against the middle; I have tried to broker changes using my special position in inappropriate ways. Usually my motives were good, but sometimes I was clearly self-serving: I wanted to be seen as key to the resolution of an issue, and in doing that abused my role. None of this is something to be proud of, but certainly something to be aware of.

Combine privileged information with trust, add power and human ambition, and you have the key ingredients of manipulation. We can end up going beyond our contracts with clients to get the results we want. The antidotes to manipulation are simpler to express than to honor. Tell people why you are dealing with them, what your purposes are. Tell them what you want from them and why. Tell them what you will do with what you learn from them, before asking for what you want. Be willing to give people as much as you are asking of them. For example, before asking where they stand on an issue, be willing to express where you stand. Let people know the means you are using to achieve the end you have in mind. Honestly express your differences with others. State your position and state theirs; point out the differences. Show your respect for positions different from your own. We can counter our own temptations to manipulate by expressing the importance of openness, by being the first to be open, by building open agreements and sticking to those agreements.

Pretense

Our work depends on accomplishment and on others' knowing about our accomplishments. We are part of a competitive consulting marketplace, and we need to be noticed to succeed. This can call out our need to bring attention to ourselves. In addition, some of us have significant needs for recognition that we bring from childhood, our school years, and our more recent life experience. These needs can lead us to pretend to be what we are not quite.

Because you are not here to offer your examples, I will offer a few of my own. I regularly catch myself in some form of pretense; it comes out in small, subtle ways. I pretend to understand more about my work than I actually understand. I nod knowingly when asked about a concept or a person in the field. Why? I want someone to be impressed with me, or at least not disappointed. Or I toss out a new piece of jargon, implying a familiarity with the ideas behind it when in fact I am ignorant. Or I exaggerate an accomplishment. Or I pretend to be doing more work or getting more money than is the truth. My motives are quite transparent when I reveal my pretense to you.

Much of the time, I am aware when I am presenting a public self that does not fit well with my private self. There are times when I even fool myself into believing that what I am saying is true, as I have done with a favorite story I have been telling for years—the story about work with a client that has the fortunate outcome of making me look good. Fifteen years ago, that story bore some resemblance to the reality from which it is derived. Today that story has been told and improved on so many times that I could not tell you what really happened if I had to! I no longer know the height of my own exaggeration. The truth has become irrelevant; what the story tells about me is all that is important. That is dangerous.

When our pretenses replace the truth, we lose our true selves in service to pretense. When we create patterns of oversimplification, exaggeration, and pretense, we risk losing track of what is real inside ourselves by pouring energy into creating a false reality outside ourselves. Our small transgressions are not my concern—if we know what we are doing. As long as we can hear that small, persistent voice saying, "What you just said is not the real truth. You know it. You are trying to fool them and impress them." This internal voice can keep us on track—or not far off track. When these reminders are not delivered, when we get so caught up in pretending that we do not hear the voice, when pretense is the pattern, then we are in trouble!

Deception

Deception is one step beyond pretense and a euphemism for lying. It took me years to acknowledge that the term often applies to me. As someone pursuing personal growth and authenticity, I know that deception is progress in the wrong direction! Yet the longer I live and the longer I do this work, the more aware I am of the differences between how I present myself and who I really am, between my public and private selves. With sixty rather than forty years behind me, I see the gap between my public and private selves narrowing and my discomfort with the gap increasing. When I am asked what concerns me most about myself, my response usually turns on deception. I struggle with being true to myself and to the people around me—clients among them.

I make excuses to myself when I choose to deceive. "They aren't ready to hear this right now." "He wouldn't like what I have to say." "She will feel badly if I tell her the truth." Isn't it good of me to protect them? Hah! Who am I really protecting? Why is it important to me to do so? My struggle is not unusual. It is a human struggle, not just this consultant's struggle. I think that our most significant growth is toward becoming our potential selves; reducing our deceptive behavior is our day-to-day, minute-to-minute opportunity to grow. And isn't that often what we are trying to help our clients do? To quit fooling themselves? When we learn to do this for ourselves, we can help them.

Here are three deception dilemmas common to my consulting. Each of them tests the boundary between authenticity and deception for me. Imagine yourself in these three situations; think about what you would do.

- You are working with a long-term client you know very well. You are uncomfortable with the amount of time it takes the two of you to plan each step in the project. You believe that your client spends too much time thinking through the details of the project, preventing both of you from thinking about the bigger picture. You also doubt that your client is presently capable of thinking in those larger terms. You have not said anything about this and have acted as if the focus on details is all right with you. In other words, you have supported the client's belief that what you are doing together is important when in fact you believe the opposite. The work has become painful to do, and you know it is so because of the issues that you have not confronted. The client knows that you are uneasy and unhappy in the work, but does not know why. What do you do?

• You are talking with a potential client. After about an hour, you are quite clear that working with this person or organization would be uncomfortable. In fact, you are sure that you do not want to work with him. He asks if you would be interested in working for him. You respond affirmatively, even enthusiastically, because you don't want him to think that you are uncomfortable with him, because you want to be liked, and because you seldom say no to new work. At this moment, you know that you would rather not work here, but you do not give him any indication of this. You don't want him to feel rejected or to think that you are judging him negatively. You want him to continue to see you as a nice person. What do you do?

• You get a call from a friend you have had for years through professional associations. She explains a situation that exists in her agency and asks you if you would be interested in consulting to the agency. You ask for more information about the project, suspecting that it does not fit well with your interests. In the process of telling you more, your friend tells you how she respects your abilities and sees you as the perfect fit for this project. At the same time, you are more sure than you were before that this project is not a good fit for you; you could do the work well enough, but it does not fit with your current interests or direction. You don't tell your friend any of your concerns because you do not want to say no to a person who obviously thinks so highly of you. Besides, she knows other friends of yours, and you want her to continue to say nice things to them about you. What do you do?

In these three cases, my concerns were not for the clients but for myself. The clients are not even aware of my dilemmas. Years of cultivating my fears, anxieties, and insecurities resulted in the deceptions I put forth. I can use my consulting to reinforce those old concerns or to challenge them. I chose to deceive these clients without involving them in that choice. I had many options available to me, many of which could have involved the clients. But I decided what they should know and could handle. I decided that they are better off not knowing the truth, that I knew best for them. I presumed that they were not strong enough to handle the truth, that their opinions, judgment, and feelings were not as important as mine. I decided they would rather know the pretending me than the real me.

We each have patterns in our struggles between authenticity and deception. We see these struggles within ourselves; we detect them going on in others. They are part of the human search for ways of being more effective and authentic in the world. When we knowingly put up a false front, we do so believing that who we really are will not be good enough; we have decided to hide behind a better image. We need to acknowledge this—at least to ourselves—before we can do anything about it. It can be quite a burden, carrying around all those false fronts and remembering which to hold up when.

Much of deception is about fooling others with the hope of fooling yourself. And if you have established strong patterns of deception, it can "work." It is often hard to know you are fooling yourself at the time; it may take years to figure out. Just think about your teenage years, and about the difference between what you were doing and what you thought you were doing. What can you do to make it less likely that you are fooling and deceiving yourself right now? Try stepping back from the situation, looking back in time, and busting your own games.

Step back from the situation. Step back from the issue at hand, reflect on life and work, move to a new perspective— all these are ways of helping us discover what we really want. All involve building in a little distance that allows for new ways of seeing. Sometimes just sleeping on the problem will do the trick. It's all about finding other ways of seeing the world; there are alternatives beyond being caught up in the moment. Most of the significant changes I see in my clients and myself involve finding a new perspective that leads to new behavior.

Look back in time. You can probably see yourself behaving in ways that would be ridiculous to you today. What do you know—over time, you have learned something! Some of that learning was quite intentional, but much of it occurred simply because you were alive and paying attention, and because time passed. A few years' perspective can often show us how we were fooling ourselves in earlier work or relationships or aspirations. This perspective often comes too late; we learn later than we would like, and this limits what we can do with the learning. Our challenge is to learn faster, to learn in months what could take years. There are ways of speeding up our learning a bit. First of all, we can just stay aware of what is going on in our lives: What is happening to us and around us, and what difference is that making to us? We need to take regular time to reflect on our life experiences and progress. There is so much I could have learned earlier if I had just known to pay attention.

Bust your own games. The way through to more honesty is conceptually both simple and threatening: reveal your true self; drop your false fronts. I get anxious just writing about it! Consultant Stan Herman has called this "busting your own games." Tell people the fronts you are carrying, the games you are playing, and how you play those games. Tell them that because you want to quit playing the game, you are revealing it to them and want them to call you on it when they see you playing. They can help you quit playing because they know it's a game that does not serve you well. Their calling you on your games decreases the likelihood that you will continue to play in your old ways.

For example, Charles meets one evening a month with six consultants to talk about work. Most of the time he works alone, so this is a unique opportunity. Through reading the earlier edition of this book, Charles came to a new awareness about himself in that consulting group: he could see himself regularly seeking attention by interjecting humor. He was quite clever, and invariably when he made a joke, people laughed, giving him some small recognition—but not really the professional recognition he wanted. In the process, he often distracted from the discussion in which they had all been involved. In busting his own game, Charles said this to the group: "I have recently realized that I need more professional recognition. In this group, I often seek that by calling attention to myself through humor. My humor can distract from our discussions—and doesn't give me the recognition I am seeking. Tell me when you think you see this happening. I will try to stop playing that game and find a more constructive way of getting what I really want."

I finish this chapter believing that most of the time we use our powers quite well. And since we are so good at addressing how our clients use their power, it is only fitting that we subject ourselves to the same scrutiny.

Part Four

Partnership

Building Long-Term Partnerships

*I*t's not enough to work with your clients; you must partner with them. Without partnership, you will end up working with an endless series of clients, rather than working often with a few clients for years. This distinction is critical to a consultant's success—at least I think so. In my most active years of consulting, there were eight organizations I worked with for between six to fourteen years. In addition to the deeper contribution and fulfillment available to me through these kinds of relationships, there was all that marketing to new clients that I did *not* have to do. This chapter discusses the key elements to forming partnerships with your clients.

Let's begin with a "formula" that provides the basis for partnership and this chapter.

Partnership is created when through time, the client's investment in your unique combination of abilities continues to equal your investment in the client's unique combination of opportunities.

Partnership is about maintaining a balance of power and interest over time. Each partner is clearly important; each needs the other for the work to be done and the partnership to continue. Both partners have power to give and receive; it is not just wielded and taken by the client or the consultant.

Let's use you as the client and me as the consultant to play out these dynamics. If I don't have any abilities you want—if I don't have any talent, liquidity, information, expertise, love, knowledge, contacts, perspective, season tickets, or position—if I don't have any abilities or connections you want, then I am power-less with you. For our relationship to work, I must have abilities you want, and you must have opportunities I want. If I have some of the abilities you want, but they also exist in the hands, heads, or hearts of many people, my power with you is reduced in direct proportion to the number of other sources you have for getting what you want. I have less power because the abilities I offer are not uniquely mine. If I am one of the only sources of the abilities you want, my power increases; I am power-full.

The same considerations and power shifting apply as I consider you, the potential client. I am looking for unique opportunities to work with you. When you offer opportunities that are unique in the marketplace and attractive to me, I am drawn to you: I know what I want; you've got it; I want to work with you! To the extent that the marketplace is long on supply of opportunities like yours, I will step back and look around; you have less power with me. But if what you offer is in short supply, I'll be drawn to you.

Clients look for this unique combination of abilities; consultants look for this unique combination of opportunities. Partnership underscores the importance of both parties' being willing to invest in their wants. It is not enough that both merely *express* their wants; action must follow for the partnership to form. The client must be willing to invest effort and time, and to take risks. The consultant must be willing to do the same. Whether we are speaking of a friendship or a client-consultant relationship, the willingness to invest is essential. The partnership is really a psychological contract in which there is a fit between opportunities and abilities. Such a relationship can be illustrated like this:

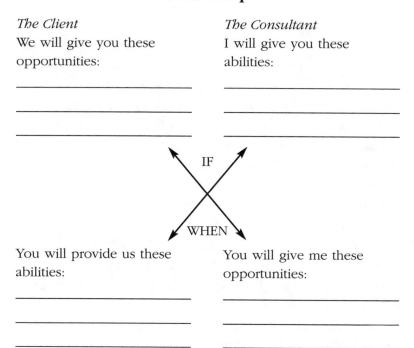

Partnership

The Client
We will give you these
opportunities:

The Consultant
I will give you these
abilities:

IF

WHEN

You will provide us these
abilities:

You will give me these
opportunities:

Notice the implied balance in this contract: neither the client nor the consultant has the advantage. The contract is not simply "You give me money, and I will deliver what you want." It goes far beyond money and results. But when we consultants hesitate to specify the abilities we possess and the opportunities we want to pursue, chances are we are defining the contract too narrowly. The better the match with the client of opportunities and abilities, the stronger the contract—and a strong contract is needed if the project hits a rough spot.

Four elements allow partnership to thrive: balance, wants, uniqueness, and fit.

Balance

As a consultant who needs clients to survive, I am especially focused on why clients choose to give power to me. From their perspective, I am a repository of abilities available to them, passive in my expression of those abilities unless they activate me. From my perspective, they are a unique set of potential opportunities, passive in their expression of those powers unless I activate them. Notice the mutuality of all this—at least as I see it. I am emphasizing balance and mutuality because I so often hear consultants speak as if they were powerless: "The client dangles the work in front of us; we take it, or . . . we take it." I do not usually see us that way; I don't like it when I occasionally act that way. I try to act from a position of power and balancing power. I don't want to start off from a "one-down" position.

Even when I know that I have the unique combination of abilities the clients want, I have a choice as to whether I will use those abilities with them. That will depend on their unique opportunities. While I am figuring this out, I remain open to the possibility of working with them; I encourage them to tell me about their work and opportunities. I must decide whether these clients have the unique, worthwhile opportunities I am looking for, while the clients are deciding whether I have the unique combination of abilities that they are looking for. My power is increased by knowing that I have a choice.

The executive vice president of a timber products company invited me in to talk with him. I had been recommended by an executive from another company. I think my name came up during a golf game. Anyhow, there I was, in the middle of balancing powers, of understanding how my wants might fit with his. I was asking lots of questions. He was answering the questions hurriedly and trying to move to discussing when I might get on a plane and fly off to work for them. Finally, in some exasperation he said, "Do you want this work or not?!" I replied, "That is exactly what I am trying to figure out!" Well, that was the end of the conversation; he was clear that he did not want to work with a consultant who worked as I was working, and I was clear that I did not want to work with him. This notion of a balance of power would not work for the two of us, and that was fine. I hope he found a consultant who gave him what he wanted. I left confident that this work was best not done by me. If I had ignored my wants and his early signals and taken the work, I would have lived to regret it, and so would he!

Wants

Regardless of who initiates contact, both you and the client have "wants." When potential clients call, you know that they want something and believe you might have it. As in my example, from the beginning we consultants are trying to establish whether the client has wants and opportunities that fit with our wants and abilities. What might we consultants have that clients might want? Here is a partial list:

Experience	Expertise	Time
Reputation	Skill	Authenticity
Age	Personality	Style
Perspective	Wisdom	Friendship
Courage	Objectivity	Accomplishment
Vision	Approval	Values
Hands	Ears	Eyes
Insight	Compassion	Products
Information	Support	Credibility

I am sure you could add to this list. Give some thought to what you would add. My list and your additions to it are your primary sources of power with clients. Partnership depends on your having something that those potential clients might want. If potential clients called right now and asked what you have to offer, what would you say?

After you have finished telling those potential clients what you offer, what would you be looking for from those potential clients? What might you want from them? Here is a partial list:

Courage	Satisfaction	Time
Accomplishment	References	Contribution
Ideas	Trust	Experience
Contract	Work	Respect
Friendship	Perspective	Risk
Money	Expertise	Wisdom
Vision	Compassion	Attention
Information	Support	Authenticity

What would you add to this list? Your decisions about which work you pursue are based on an intuitive list you are already keeping. Why not make it more explicit by writing it down and prioritizing it? I am betting that you will learn something in the process.

My lists of what I want and what my clients want overlap. Surprising? Perhaps not. There is much that my clients and I might both want. Five of the wants listed are particularly important to me and to my clients: expertise, perspective, authenticity, friendship, and accomplishment (more about these in Chapters Six and Seven).

Uniqueness

My abilities must be unique enough and obvious enough that clients will be attracted to me among others. Somehow, I must distinguish myself from other consultants. If I offer what others offer, in the way others offer it, I will get the same opportunities as everyone else. In other words, I will be excluded from special opportunities for a good reason: I have nothing special to offer. I must define my uniqueness through the combination of abilities I possess.

Your uniqueness defines you in the mind of the client, but it is just as important for you to define your uniqueness for yourself, so that the work you take more likely fits with who you are. We consultants working alone (rather than in a large firm) have the special opportunity to be professionally unique in personal ways. Our challenge is to find the unique combination of abilities in our work that reflects who we are as individuals. Large firms market themselves by showing potential clients their unique character; we little firms should too. The difference is that the "personality" being defined is our own rather than that of a big firm.

A cautionary tale: Fred struck out on his own as a consultant eight years ago. He had been struggling to get started for about a year when a client discovered Fred's background in getting unions decertified and hired him in that capacity. Fred's success with this client led to other clients and a few articles in national publications. Today Fred is prosperous, and his very successful firm of many consultants is busily engaged in breaking unions around the world. Fred's unique talent, widely requested and well paid for, has defined a special niche for him.

Wonderful? Not so wonderful. The uniqueness that defines Fred's firm does not fit with who Fred is and what he wants to do. Have a drink with Fred and hear him lament his success at doing something he really doesn't want to do. He complains about his travel schedule; he gripes about having to deliver one message over and over, a message he is no longer invested in. Fred successfully defined a uniqueness that is not what he really wants to stand for and do. He lives as if decertifying unions is the most important thing to him, while what is truly important to him goes unexplored. Fred plays a role that does not fit with who he is.

Fit

Our clients look at many consultants with résumés comparable to our own. I often ask clients why they chose me; their answer often includes the word *match* or *chemistry* or *fit*. They see my style as matching their own; my uniqueness complements their uniqueness. They believe they will be comfortable with the way I will work with them. Clients who have just chosen me seldom say, "We needed this project done by this date, and you said you could do it," or "Your fees were lower than others," or "You had the best résumé." There are plenty of consultants with the abilities they need, but they need something beyond that; they need fit.

While they are going through those considerations, so am I. I am checking to see whether I have the skills this client needs, whether I like the people, whether we can talk, whether I will likely succeed—whether this project is a good fit.

Fit has to do with being on the same wavelength— with seeing the world, the people, and the organization in similar ways. Fit has to do with behaving in ways the organization behaves; respecting similar values; working toward related, long-term goals; reinforcing each other's contributions and comments; respecting the way things are done in the organization; and being mutually critical of how things are done in the organization. Fit suggests more agreement than disagreement on how to approach the issues at hand and what might be done about them. Most of all, fit is personal, and all parties sense it. Good fit provides the basis for learning and risking together; it's an important element of building trust. Without fit, change is very difficult.

As much attention as clients pay to fit, I usually pay more. I know well how much it costs me in stress and strain to work with people or on a project where I do not feel there is a good fit. My earlier story with the executive vice president demonstrates my concern. Nevertheless, it is possible for me to work with clients when there is not a good fit; I do so probably 20 percent of the time—not because I was not checking but because I misread the situation. Poor fit does not automatically spell disaster for a project; it just means more energy expended, more discomfort for me and my clients. When I get stuck with a bad fit, I seldom jump ship. Instead, I remind myself that I chose these clients and that I am there only part-time. The clients have enough problems already without having to deal with special problems coming from their overly sensitive consultant. I am used to adapting to organizations—more used to it than they are to adapting to consultants—so I try to do that . . . and then leave at the first opportunity when I can show success on a completed piece of work.

My emphasis on the softer side of long-term partnerships in no way diminishes the importance of expertise to our success. But without balance, wants, uniqueness, and fit, partnership will be short-lived.

Making Rewarding Partnerships

While thinking back over my partnerships with clients, I met with consultants and asked for their experiences of what has worked and not worked for them. I combined their ideas with mine to come up with two lists: the "good news" and "bad news" of partnership. Before reading these lists, jot down a few notes for yourself. What patterns do you see in the high and low spots in your relationships with clients? When I gave time to thinking about this, I made some useful discoveries; perhaps you will too. We will look at the good news now and get to the bad news in the next chapter. Here is what we consultants came up with, supplemented with some of my personal experiences. Following this discussion, I will talk about the key to successful partnerships: clear contracting.

The Good News

We share a vision of the work. That vision guides day-to-day decisions and is always more important than the plans put in place to realize the vision. Not only is the vision shared but so is the energy behind it. It helps if the work is mutually viewed as something of a pioneering effort. Together, we intend to cross the mountains we see in the distance; we are ready to face the deserts, rivers, and forests that must be crossed to get there. Just thinking about what we intend to do together excites us.

We all know this is important work. The larger the circle of "investors," the better. For example, working with a hospital management team has a positive potential outcome for the team, but also for the patients, the staff, the community, the insurers, and the medical profession as a whole. This greater buy-in lends energy to the project; everyone who is part of it knows it is important. I recently spent a day with managers from a cancer research facility. The sense of duty to humankind and of the importance of their work was palpable. This makes for good work and good partnerships.

We work within a structure. Being highly enthused about an important project is not nearly enough. We need a plan, model, or structure that we follow in deciding what to do when. This framework will be the container for our aspirations, enthusiasm, energy, and talent. For example, I helped a plant and its leadership team develop a design for the plant of the future—the kind of plant they intended to become. Over the next four years, all of their plant redesign work was in relation to the larger framework they had created. Along the way, as they learned more, they adjusted the framework and the actions within it, but they always honored the frame. Quarterly offsite sessions always included a look into how the framework was working.

We value results above activity. Each meeting of the partners is outcome oriented. And each outcome contributes to the larger vision or model. We know what we are going to do today and how it will move us forward. All partners think in terms of delivering results, even in their briefest encounters.

We talk regularly. Communication is in both directions. We talk about what is working well and what is not; we remind ourselves of what we are trying to do and how we each can help. Everyone intends to keep everyone else current. Face-to-face meetings are essential and supplemented with voice and electronic data. We are all confident that we are informed, and we are comfortable contacting anyone at any time.

We see each other as partners. We all expect to work, contribute, make mistakes, and succeed together. We mutually acknowledge the expectation to both learn and contribute. Although all partners are experienced, we also know that we cannot do this work alone; we each intend to rely on others. Partnership includes a willingness to explore, to take risks, to assess problems, and to celebrate success.

Our work is more important than our roles. Defining roles is a useful starting point, but what is more compelling to each partner is what needs to be done now—regardless of role. Good work together is supported primarily by a common vision and common aspirations, rather than by confining definitions of who does what. Roles are readily put aside whenever the situation calls for it.

We fit. My consultant friends and I underline the point made repeatedly in this book. Partners need more than a

meshing of technical skills or authority. In the best partnerships, they converse easily. Understanding between
partners goes beyond what has been said; the partners find
each other interesting. There is even the possibility of a
friendship that could extend beyond work.

The clients do the important work. Better yet, they want
to do the work. They see the consultant as an adviser, guide,
helper, and coach. They know that if the project is to succeed, it cannot be done for them; it must be done by them.
They take deep ownership of the work and its outcomes.

Clear Contracting Between Us

Not far in the background of each of these expressions of
rewarding partnership is the deal that makes it all possible:
the emerging agreement between client and consultant, the
understanding they hold in common about what each will
do, when and where they will do it, and with what expected
outcomes. Contracting is often what allows relationships to
succeed; poor contracting is often the cause of their failure—
a point we will take up again in Chapter Seventeen.

No step is more important to the consulting process
than contracting. Contracting is an exchange of wants and
needs, and we and our clients need to be clear about what
each expects of the other and what each is going to provide
the other. The agreement we reach initially with our clients
is the first of an emergent series of agreements that regularly
change and adapt to current circumstances. The contract
starts with first contact and is alive, and being renegotiated,
throughout the entire consulting relationship. Either person
can open a discussion of this living contract at any time.

Contracting as I write about it here is related to, but
also significantly different from, a legal contract. Contracting

is a dynamic, not a document. Certainly you may choose to "freeze" the current understandings in a written contract, but that is not likely to capture the continuing life of the agreement between you. A legal document, once it is finished, is more dead than alive. Contracts that emphasize this written form may miss the substance of the client-consultant partnership.

Legalistic contracts have the same effect on partnerships with clients that prenuptial agreements have on marriages. Even when necessary, they are not very romantic, nor are they what the partnership is primarily about. I avoid written contracts when possible; I negotiate them when necessary. I attempt to create a contracting process with my clients that is alive and adaptable, not one that is fixed in ink. I encourage trust between client and consultant. I see anything that smacks of mistrust—as defensive legal contracts can—as damaging to the partnership I want to establish. I favor written communication that records what we decided so that we don't forget our responsibilities. I keep files that track the work the client and I are doing together, but I balk at anything written that suggests we are protecting ourselves from each other.

Clients occasionally require some form of contract of me, and I am usually willing to sign what they put together. I'm not ornery about it; I just don't encourage the practice by focusing on such documents. If a signature is required, I'll sign. If the legal contract begins to intrude on our work discussions, I get concerned. I have signed perhaps twelve contracts in twenty years of consulting. Your work may have different requirements; my approach has worked for me.

At the same time, I must acknowledge that most of the major problems I had when I was a client, and that I have had as a consultant, can be traced back to poor contracting.

Many of the problems detailed in Chapter Seventeen link back to poor contracting. I hasten to add that the problems I had would not have been solved by a legalistic document. Instead I would criticize my lack of clarity, inattention to detail, failure to keep up with changes, or misunderstanding of the other person's intentions. Many consultants are more structured and contract oriented in their dealings with their clients, and it works well for them. I am not suggesting that they stop, but rather that they reconsider the necessity.

How do I reconcile my need for a living contract with the need for a written memory of what we are doing together? Following a lengthy discussion or negotiation with a client, I often write a letter or e-mail outlining the major points discussed and what we each plan to do. This confirms the points on which we agreed and the actions we will take and gives us a record of what transpired between us.

Starting work with a new partner is similar to dancing with someone you have never danced with before. You and this new dance partner do not have to go through a long negotiation about when you are going to dance, who is going to lead or follow, how long you will dance, whether you will dance again, or what will happen if you do not like dancing together. No, you start with some positive assumptions and limited commitment and work from there. You learn how to dance with each other by paying close attention while you dance. You learn from each other starting from where you are, and as the relationship proceeds and deepens, you adjust to it and talk about it.

As I've said, contracting happens not only at the start of the client-consultant dance but throughout the work together. In the past, it was important to me to regularly stop working to talk about how things were going. More

often now, I check in with my partner while we are working. I begin the partnership and contracting with a larger
number of positive assumptions about how the client and
I will work together and tend to put fewer concrete details
in the initial contracting process. I want to see how this
partnership will work by *doing* it, not by planning it. I try
to ensure that the two of us understand what will happen
between our starting point and our future destination and
worry less about the specifics of what will happen as we
travel there. (Often enough we won't even get there, or the
destination we originally selected will change.) Clients are
drawn to the idea of getting right to work; they like that
aspect of this approach. We get more work done, and our
contracting is more relevant and timely.

Seventeen

Avoiding Painful Partnerships

$\mathcal{W}$ hen my consultant friends discussed what causes partnerships to fail, suffer, or just be frustrating, they came up with a long list. We all had lots of experience in partnering poorly. Much of the time the clues were there in the beginning, especially for the more experienced consultants. Some of us persisted in making the same mistakes over and over; those patterns are particularly important to watch for. Here is our list; compare it to your own.

The contracting is unclear. Some of us continue to refuse to learn the message of the closing point of Chapter Sixteen. We find partway down the road with our clients that what we have contracted to do is not what is needed or is not what we are actually doing. Or our work with the clients is not going well because we are operating from different understandings of our agreement. Or we are clear about the outcomes intended, but differ so much in our values that we cannot work well together; in other words, although we think we know what we are going to do together, we do not know how we are going to do it or why it is important. This last problem is a personal favorite of mine. In my quest for creating informal relationships with clients, I often neglect getting formal clarity.

You work your own agenda. If as consultant you come into the work with too much foreknowledge, you enter the partnership "knowing better" than the client right from the start. You know so much, there is no need to pay close attention; you can just do what you already know will work. Don't bother with what the client wants; give them what you know they need. This is a big mistake, and I have made it numerous times. Even when the work turned out well, I was not invited back to do more. I lost sight of who was sponsoring me and the need to respect the client's wants.

The fit is poor. Other parts of this book emphasize fit between consultant and client. Both good and bad experiences cause me to underline this point. Even when the work is worthwhile, if there is a poor fit, you will be reminded of your bad "marriage" every day. For example, I was being pursued by someone who wanted me to work for his company. For some reason, I didn't like him and tried to avoid the opportunity to work with him. But I listened to his explanation of the work, and it sounded interesting. Hmmm. . . . Perhaps if I asked for more money than usual, he would either go away or hire me and in effect pay me for the extra trouble. He offered me the work on my higher terms, I accepted, and I suffered through. But I was wrong: it was a deal not worth doing. And the mistake was mine, not his. There is just no point in encouraging someone to use me when I don't want to work with that person.

The client has too much work and too little money. Trying to operate within tight financial boundaries dampens the whole project. No one feels free to think expansively. When I take on such confined work, I spend more time on the project than I get paid for, and I end up resenting the client because I decided to take on the work. Sometimes clients sense this, and sometimes I tell them—which complicates our dynamics and takes even more time that I am not paid for.

The project becomes less important to the client. After a decent beginning, the project starts slipping off track. The track is constantly changed. Meetings are rescheduled. I am kept waiting. The client ends up paying me to sit around and wait. All of these are symptoms of slippage. In retrospect, I can see the seeds of this slippage planted as far back as our initial contracting. My responsibility is to tell the client what I see happening and how I interpret its meaning, and to get the client's response.

You accept work you would not ordinarily do. For me, this usually happens during a bout of financial anxiety. I wish I could commit to never doing it again, but no promises! The main reason I accept the wrong kind of work is that I allow myself to be seduced. The prospective clients say nice things about me or my work; they talk about how special my talents are; they say I'm someone they would like to work with sometime. I act modest, say it would be nice to work together—and replay their every word for three weeks. Months later they call. They tell me again how wonderful my work is and remind me that I said I would like to work with them. Then they ask to meet to talk about a project they are working on. We do that, and in the process of trying to look wonderful, I agree to do something for them that doesn't really fit with what I want to do. It's not their fault that I choose to do this.

You go after the money. One of the worst reasons to take on work is for the money. If that is one of the main reasons you are working for a client, you will likely find the work a struggle. Not that working for money is evil; it isn't. But there are higher motivations, and they serve you better over the long haul. So why do I go after the money at least once a year? I am feeling anxious or underappreciated, there are blank spots on the calendar where work ought to be, and I think I need money. Somebody calls, and I respond affirmatively before she asks the question. Money gets in the way of work; it distracts from serving clients well. I should be asking myself whether I can serve them well, not whether I need the money.

You catch the client's "disease." Some clients carry "illnesses" that are too close to our own, resulting in our becoming part of the organization's problem. The illnesses afflicting the organization begin to show up in us, and we begin behaving in the same less effective ways that it behaves.

Let me give you an example. In the midst of a large project with an insurance company, a design team and I were working on an identified problem: people in the organization were highly averse to taking risks. The reasons were many, including fear of losing their jobs, fear of the key executives, and fear of rejection. Our preparation to put this issue before the organization took one meeting, two meetings, three meetings. I began to get very uncomfortable. We just couldn't decide together on an approach that we all supported. We found ourselves bound up in details and trying to provide for every contingency. And I was not being very helpful; I was as stuck as everyone else, and I wasn't talking to the team about my discomfort. I figured we were already spending too much time on this, so why spend even more on my problems?

It was about then that I figured it out: I had caught the disease. The reason we couldn't put a plan together was that we were afraid: afraid of getting fired, afraid of the key executives, afraid that our good ideas would be rejected. Our issues weren't out there in the organization; they were in here, in this team, in us, in me. I was in effect supporting their risk-avoidance behaviors. My actions reinforced the idea that this was a fearful place to work, that it was those people out there we had to watch out for, and that we couldn't do a lot about the situation— not very helpful. I am more aware of my susceptibility to others' maladies now, but I have not developed an immunity or found a booster shot that protects me. Catching the disease still screws up my work. I become one of the afflicted in the organization, and they end up paying me to solve problems I have rather than to focus on problems they have. Illness here is only a metaphor, but it seems particularly apt.

You hold naive positive assumptions. Ordinarily, positive assumptions about people serve us well, but not when they lead us to expect people to do something they are completely unprepared to do. What happens when you act as though people can do something that they can't? They are unwilling to disappoint you or themselves; they often don't tell you they are in trouble. When their piece of the work runs aground, special effort is required to help them—perhaps more effort than it would have taken to prepare them well in the first place. We need to make it easy for others to say, "I don't know how" or "I need help." Recognizing my pattern of making naive positive assumptions has moved me toward more consciously assessing people's skills.

You pretend. There is something going on that the client is not talking about. And you aren't talking about it either. It is important, and you both know you are avoiding it. Together you act as if the situation is not there, finding ways to fool yourselves and not bring it up.

I was working with the executive committee of a company in the computer industry. The work involved redefining the company's mission and direction, supporting that with a change strategy that eventually involved everyone in the company in looking at the company's mission, direction, philosophy, and values. The CEO of the company was sleeping with the vice president of finance and married to someone else. Everybody knew it and, further, believed that the VP was being favored at work. This behavior also conflicted with one of the new values of the company. When the CEO talked to groups about the company's direction and values, his speeches were not very believable. The relationship between these two executives was undermining important company efforts. Everyone, including me, was pretending.

This is a dramatic example of the pretenses in which we can get caught up. We were all pretending we did not know about their affair. Once I became aware of my pretense, I figured out what to do about it. After talking with a few people, I stopped pretending and told the CEO what was being openly discussed across the organization. I linked the behavior to company values and leadership. I left all this information with the CEO, and we never discussed it again. What happened to the relationship? I don't know. I do know that they had the information about how their relationship affected the organization, and they knew that others knew. And I was no longer pretending.

Many of the contributions to painful partnerships stem from personal weaknesses that show up in the partnership. This suggests that the work begins with ourselves, our clarity, our authenticity, and our willingness to express to our partners what we know ourselves.

Part Five

Understanding Organizations

Eighteen

How Organizations Work

*O*rganizations hire us, use us, exalt us, abuse us, feed us, and sometimes consume us. We serve them our time and talent in hopes of making a living and a difference. Each school system, corporation, neighborhood, social service agency, governmental body, church, and foundation works toward its purpose with its people within its structures; each develops defining characteristics. All organizations work to contain their resources, to channel them to unique purpose. This is the challenge, the magic, the madness, and the mystery that make organizations so fascinating. And there is so much we do not know about them.

We Know Little About Organizations

"In the beginning, God created organizations." No, this is not the way Genesis begins. Organizations came along later—probably as a little trick God played on us. The organizations most of us serve are a more recent human creation. Stretch out an arm; imagine that the length of your outstretched arm represents human time on Earth, starting at your shoulder and extending to the end of your pointing index finger. Large organizations came into being somewhere near the end of your fingernail—and consultants arrived almost simultaneously! Large organizations are a recent phenomenon in human history. They have existed for around five thousand years; we have been studying and writing about them for maybe five hundred years. Most of that study and writing has been in the last one hundred years, and there is still much we do not know about how organizations work. What we do not know about them far surpasses what we do know. This suggests that we must approach them with respect, curiosity, and humility— respect because they are awesome in their complexity and power, curiosity because they provide wonderful opportunities to learn, and humility because the forces at work within them truly humble us.

Clients often hire us because they think we "know"; they think we understand organizations. Perhaps you think you understand, but I know that I do not. When I am at my best, I make my living by proclaiming what I do not understand and seeking further understanding. That is what all the meetings, interviews, listening, reports, and discussions are about: developing a deeper shared understanding of what is happening in this organization.

Organizations are large, awkward, and unwieldy. People put them together so that other people can pool their talents to produce goods and services. Usually organizations don't work very well, because they don't fit the human creatures who work in them. We struggle to help organizations work; we have no choice but to continue that struggle if we want to keep living in the world we have built around ourselves. We are right to constantly question the structures that contain people's labors, for surely there are always alternative ways to use people's talents better, to meet people's life purposes better, within an organization that delivers products or services the world needs.

We have built organizations that are more mechanical than "organical." We have lost the "organ" in organization as we have built awkward hierarchical structures with boxes and lines connecting them. Consider similarly rooted words, such as *organ, organism, orgasm, orgy,* and *organic.* Funky, damp, fertile words teeming with life! Organizations contain that life too, but too often our structures and systems seem designed to wring the life out of the place. Instead of creating rich, life-filled, working organisms, we often create structures modeled after machines—mechanistic, repetitious, predictable, and inflexible—that wedge moving human parts into cogs and corners. Our structures serve only some of the needs of the people who make them run. These structures should be in service to their entire workforce, their community, their vendors, their marketplace, and the environment, not just their customers and stockholders. Our challenge is to find ways of creating organizations that will better serve all the people invested in them.

Organizations Do Not Work

Years ago during a workshop, we had just spent thirty minutes hearing participants talk about problems in their respective organizations. We had heard a passionate display of ranting and raving against organizations. I interrupted our complaining to say, "Raise your hand if you work for an organization that is basically pretty screwed up." About twenty-five of thirty people raised their hands.

We were silent for a moment . . . then we all began to laugh, long and hard. The message was clear: it is "screwed up" almost everywhere! And if any particular organization isn't screwed up now, it used to be or soon will be! That is the reality of organization life. Our ranting and raving held the implication that our various organizations should be perfect, that each of them was the exception to some larger norm of perfection. The raised hands said no, it's like this everywhere. The laughter suggested our need to recognize and accept the reality we begin with. Understanding this gave us a great relief and release—and opened us to acceptance.

In this imperfect world full of imperfect people, we try to get things done through large, imperfect organizations— organizations of our own creation. These organizations attempt to bring together a complex combination of resources to meet a wide array of often conflicting needs. Such organizations do not work very well. Even when everyone and everything is finely attuned to what the organization is about, there are significant difficulties. Where is it written that a five-tiered organization of ten thousand people across fifty states and twenty product lines should be without strife? Or even an untiered structure of thirty people, all networked and connected, delivering one service? The assumptions underlying our discomfort with organizations are often downright laughable. It's as if we really expect them to work! And we are astonished when they do not! What is truly astonishing is that we get so much done through these awkward systems and structures. That we do is a great testimony to the human spirit and the need to find meaning in our lives; we seek meaning even when surrounding structures try to preclude it.

It is so easy to point at what is wrong and much more difficult to find out what's right. We routinely hear ourselves and others talk about what a hard week we are having, or the killer meeting this morning, or how unreasonable our client is, or . . . The list goes on and on. Granted, it is a hard week, the meeting was tough, and so is the client. But why do we keep talking about it? The organization continues to offer us opportunities to talk about what's screwed up, broken, not working, and stupid. We continue to rant and expect much more of the organization than it delivers. Consider the unspoken assumption behind the patterned complaints you hear in an organization; it is often "This place should be perfect." Organizations aren't perfect, and they never will be. Neither are you, and neither am I. Our expectations about our clients and ourselves ought to accept our human limitations—even as we work to improve. We need to recognize that these imperfect organizational and human forms cannot deliver the perfection we seek. We need to build in a certain amount of tolerance and forgiveness.

Organizations Don't Make Sense

Much of what happens in organizations and in our own lives does not make much sense; it isn't all that logical, rational, or linear. We talk as if what we do in our lives makes sense, as if we do what we do because we are reasonable. I used to believe this, but I don't any longer. Oh, certainly there are many actions we take each day that make sense, but most of them are not very important. When something important happens in our lives, our commitment and investment go beyond the rational. We bring more of ourselves to it. Your head sensibly builds a "to do" list, or decides when to get your car serviced or what time to call a client, but none of these decisions is very important. You can let your head take care of them. But when it comes to deciding whether to be a consultant, where to live, who to marry, whether to have a child—these decisions are too big for your head to handle alone. You must reach beyond your rational faculties for guidance.

My wife and I talked recently about our big decisions of the last thirty-six years, and we could not find one that was primarily rational. Getting married, having children, choosing where to work, going to graduate school, becoming a consultant, moving to Seattle—none of these decisions relied primarily on our rational faculties. Certainly we had a rationale for each decision, but that usually came after the decision. Consider the big decisions you have made in your life. How many of them were purely rational?

Given that organizations are collections of people, most important organizational decisions are not made because they are logical and rational. Logic and rationality are used in support of decisions, as a kind of psychic insurance. Every day you can see people on television or in the press explaining why they did what they did. As you listen to them, you are hearing their rationalization for doing what they wanted to do.

There is so much in organizations that does not make sense; let's quit pretending that it does. Organizations swing through cycles of centralization and decentralization; they don't do it because it makes sense. Executives are often selected first of all for loyalty and secondarily for expertise. That doesn't make sense! People with greater responsibility are often given larger offices; those with less responsibility get small cubicles. That doesn't make sense! Meeting after meeting begins late, drags on without an agenda, wastes time, and ends late. That doesn't make sense! Much of business and life does not make sense, and I am not arguing that it should. Instead I am arguing against pretending that it should. Let's accept the idea that much of what we call rational is really rationalization—the logical excuses we make for doing what we really want to do or for doing what someone else wants us to do.

Accept Organizational "Non-Sense"

One of the best ways to stress yourself out or to get sick is to expect organizations to be rational. Demand that they make sense! Ask them to be logical! Require that they be reasonable! And expect ulcers! Or you can accept the non-sense. To accept does not mean that you *agree;* it means that you see what is going on and are willing to accommodate that reality. Accept that this executive's pet project will be pursued—even if it does not make sense. Accept that these two guys don't like each other and will not work together no matter how much sense it might make for them to do so. Accept this team's fear of bringing forth new ideas, or that person's overzealous pursuit of personal goals. Each of these common behaviors goes beyond the rational and is asking you for acceptance. These behaviors—along with thousands of others—define what an organization is really about and ask for you to understand.

The organizational upside of all this irrationality is that people can bring more informed energy and focus to their work than reason could ever demand. They bring the motivation we are so often seeking. The organizational down-side is that people can use their less rational selves to restrict their energies, to misdirect or twist the ways they invest themselves. There is no way of accepting the upside and rejecting the downside; they are two sides of the same phenomenon. What differences do exist are in our perception. When people are doing what we want them to be doing, we see that as positive; we see the opposite as negative. Truly exceptional organizational behavior depends on the right kind of irrationality.

Are you running around client organizations muttering, "This doesn't make sense!" "They are so unreasonable!" "Logically, they ought to . . ."? If you have a pattern of behaving in these "rational" ways, and it is accompanied by headaches, chest pains, stomach pains, or constipation, then maybe it is time for you to take a look at your expectations of your clients. Demanding that people be reasonable and logical is a tremendous drain on you, especially if the demands are not being met. To accept clients as they are is to be on a different path from the one you take when you attempt to impose order on them. Accepting people as they are brings mystery, intrigue, passion, confusion, and out-and-out craziness. Taking the path of acceptance means loosening your hold on rationality and, perhaps more threatening, releasing the reins of control. When you accept that people will behave in ways that don't make sense to you, you have opened yourself to an overwhelming array of options, an array that goes far beyond what the rational can offer.

Let reason be your guide, not your dictator. It is one of a number of guides, all offering their services to us. Intuition is also a guide. So is emotion. So is the heart. So is spirit. In organizations, reason is too often the only acknowledged guide. We force emotionally based insight to enter in the guise of reason, rather than accepting it for what it is. We can assist our clients in understanding the guides they are following. We can help them explore what is reasonable and logical, and how that is related to their emotional investment in the situation. We can help them legitimize both "This is what makes sense" and "This is what we want." We can help them do what they want to do without pretending that it makes sense. We can help them avoid doing something that makes sense that they don't want to do.

What Organizations Want Most Cannot Be Measured

This contrary bit of wisdom has helped me sort my way through many organizations. I know that if I am to help my clients, I must work on what is deeply important to them; they will not bring energy to anything except their high priorities. The prevailing "wisdom" of organization life—especially the for-profit world—says that if you cannot measure it, it is not important. I disagree. I believe that if it is important, you cannot measure it. The most important things in life cannot be measured, made tangible, quantified, packaged, boxed, or tied down. In fact, the most important things in life are not *things* at all. What we want out of life is not for sale, for lease, or for rent.

Consider the man and woman who have been dating for three years and were engaged six months ago. Today they are marrying in a big ceremony with their families and friends in attendance. They have been looking forward to this moment for a long time. They feel a deep love for each other as they commit to living the rest of their lives together. Neither of them can think of anything more important that has ever happened to them. Consider the members of an agency board that successfully created a vision of what they want their little organization to become. They have also created a common understanding of what their mutual role is in bringing this vision to reality. They are all emotionally inspired by what they have done together, and their spirits are higher than they have ever been; they are excited about the future they are going to create. Consider a work team of five that set aside a half-day to look at alternative ways of doing its work and redesign its work process and individual roles. The team members are thrilled with their accomplishment.

We could ask the people in these three situations to complete questionnaires, submit to interviews, and report to us on what they have done together and how they felt about what they have done. The data could be useful to us as indicators of what happened but would not capture what happened. The only way to know fully what happened would be to experience it. Everything else directed toward the experience is a poor attempt at capturing it. These efforts may be the best we can do, but that does not make them effective. Counter to the bottom-line fixation of the widget-watchers of the Western world, the essence of our most meaningful experiences is not quantifiable, measurable, or tangible. Yes, we can collect quantifiable data related to the experience, but those data are different from the experience itself. We cannot put calipers on a dream, on happiness, on excitement, on motivation. The essence is found through being in the experience, not standing outside measuring it. As useful as measurement might be, it remains outside the world it is assessing. And we forget that. We confuse the measurement with the experience.

We consultants and clients lose track of why we are measuring what we are measuring; we just do not ask why enough. Instead we concentrate on what, when, where, and how. We know what to do and how to do it, and we just do the job, over and over again. With time, the why question fades from our minds and hearts. We look around us at work and see others busily engaged in doing the same thing, so how wrong could we be? We measure ourselves against them, or what we did last year, or what we plan to do this year, but not against the question, Why? We measure what is easier to measure rather than what is important. Some of us begin to think that our measures are important; we lose sight of what they were designed to support. If you find yourself bound up in the measurable or tied up with numbers, you need to remember that these things are simply indicators pointing to what is truly important. We have created all these numbers to keep track of it—whatever "it" is.

If you find yourself working to achieve something measurable for its own sake, without regard for what it is contributing to, know that you have narrowed yourself and blocked other, larger perspectives. This is your clue to ask, Why? If you find yourself arguing with a client that the numbers are not what is most important, you are on the right track but need to question your methods. Do not argue against measurement and numbers; argue *for* using measurement as an indicator. For example, this quarter's profits can be celebrated because they are an indicator of corporate health and movement toward purpose. Money becomes an indicator rather than a goal in itself. Do not ignore the numbers your client respects. Help the client see what those numbers indicate; search for other indicators that also answer the question, Why? The deepest answers will be more descriptive than quantitative. Then you probably will have reached the dreams, the vision, the values of the organization that are most important. These are what the numbers try unsuccessfully to capture.

As our clients are bombarded with requests for measurements of what they are achieving, they lose their sense of organizational purpose and life direction. But who are we to shake our heads and cluck about our client's lost perspective? We have that same difficulty ourselves, and we must always strive to remember what is important (and unmeasurable) in our own lives.

Organizations Change Slowly

Despite my years of experience with helping organizations change, I have regularly helped organizations underestimate what it takes to change. I have helped them oversimplify what can be accomplished and how to go about the work. My best guesses usually fall far short of what is actually required in time, energy, and dollars to bring about major change. And my estimates are far larger than the ones my clients usually come up with. What I think will require three years, they think might take a year—and it actually takes five years. We all have a lot to learn.

One of the main reasons change efforts falter or fail is that most people do not know what they are signing up for when they begin. We must let go of our naive assumptions and our need for immediate action. Here is a typical experience: I watched and helped guide a client through a total organizational redirection and restructuring. Thousands of lives were affected: hundreds of families relocated, many people retired, and hundreds of roles were redefined. The amount of energy, time, talent, and money expended on this effort far exceeded what was anticipated when we began. Six years later, the organization has still not regained a balance resembling the one it held before all this change began. This is not an argument against the change; it is just a recognition that we did not know what we were getting into. There must be very compelling reasons to engage in organizational change of this magnitude. We need to help our clients understand the immensity of their undertakings before they commit to them. We need to learn much more deeply the truth about changing these huge creatures called organizations.

Respect the Organization for What It Is

Consider any organization you work with today. Many people worked very hard to bring it to where it is today. This organization reached this point because of the intentions of tens or hundreds or thousands of people throughout its history. Whatever shape it is in right now is because of the work of those people. No, all those people did not want the organization to arrive at the position it is in today, but every one of them did contribute. Respect the energy, the intelligence, the sweat, the motivation, the spirit, and the intention that has gone into bringing the organization to this point. And yes, respect the well-intentioned mistakes, the misguided failures, the human foibles, the ulcers, and the tears that are part of where the organization is now. For better or for worse, many people have worked very hard to bring the organization to this moment.

While we anticipate a future that we can only dream of, we usually build on the past we have already experienced. The resources (financial, natural, human, information, physical) that brought the organization to where it is are often needed to move it forward. Maybe those resources will be supplemented, maybe they will be used differently, but much of what is needed to move the organization toward its aspirations is in the organization right now. Our challenge is to help our clients find it, uncover it, transform it, align it, or use it.

What can we consultants do and not do to show our respect for the history and the mystery of our client organizations? When we act as if nothing worthwhile happened before our arrival on the scene, we are risking the loss of essential support. When we discount the people who have invested years creating the present organization, we are making enemies where we need friends. When we start by suggesting that revolutionary change is required, we may be demonstrating how little we understand. We would do better to seek understanding of the organization's history and the people who contributed to it. Ask them to talk about it. Learn about the historical foundation on which the organization will build its future. When we avoid assigning blame and instead attempt to understand, we serve ourselves well. Part of respecting history is spending time in it. When we make a special effort to find out what has gone on in the past, we gain allies. Files and reports give us the dusty background on how the organization has operated, but face-to-face contact with the people immerse us in its rich history. Meet the people, hear their stories, and learn their culture. You will find yourself more deeply engaged with what is happening here. You will get a privileged peek into the enormity and the complexity of what makes this organization work.

Nineteen

What Works When Creating Change

*C*onsulting and change are joined at the hip. This work may be most connected to building the effectiveness of organizations, systems, and people, but such building usually means change. The world is moving so fast that even to stay in place, we have to change. Just ask your clients what they were thinking about when they hired you or your firm: change. Ask the people throughout the organization who might be affected by your work what you mean to them: change—and anxiety. Here are a few of the many ways to focus change in people and organizations. Consider which you use.

Focus of Change

ABILITIES: Knowledge, skills, habits, feelings
CONCEPTS: Models, frameworks, ideas
PROCESSES: Systems, procedures
DIRECTION: Goals, mission, purpose, objectives
BOUNDARIES: Standards, tolerance, parameters

INTENTIONS: Aspirations, motives, needs
CONSEQUENCES: Rewards, punishment, reinforcement,
    extinguishers
PERSPECTIVE: Vision, viewpoint, position
CONTEXT: Environment, culture, norms
ENLIGHTENMENT: Wisdom, value, belief, myth

Think about other consultants and their approaches;
you will find them focusing more on some of these categories than others. Some of us place our faith and effort in
abilities, believing that if we change what people are able
to do, that will have an impact on the organization. Others
of us rely on clear *boundaries,* believing that when people
know the standards to be met, they can perform within
those standards. Others of us would focus on clear *direction* or *consequences.* Of course, all of us use some combination of these categories to bring about the changes our
clients want.

Just as I have seen patterns in the focus of change categories listed here, I have also seen patterns in what works
and does not work for me when I am trying to bring about
change. The world of organizations is a hard teacher; it
offers you experience but does not sit you down to tell
you what to learn from that experience. You have to do
that for yourself. With a few years of experience, some success and failure, you will see some patterns emerge. You
may or may not be paying attention, but the patterns are
there. The sooner you pick up on them, the more effective
you will be.

Years ago, I put together a short list of "consulting
wisdom" that guides me in my day-to-day work. I learned
from my patterns; I learned from other people's. I can
recall most of this wisdom from memory; it keeps me on
track—when I follow it. Taken together, all this wisdom

defines the kind of consultant I want to be. As you review the consulting wisdom I have developed, think about your own: What guides you? What have you learned about clients, organizations, change, and yourself that serves you particularly well? Note your ideas, and if any of mine really strike home, you can add them to your list. Let's begin.

The Work Begins Here and Now

There is simply no place else to start. As obvious as that may sound to you, it certainly is not always that obvious to me. I frequently want my clients to be more ready, more relaxed, more visionary than they are. I sometimes blame them for being who they are instead of who I want them to be. But I am missing the point when I get caught in those fantasies: the work begins here and now! Reminding myself of that grounds me and engages my action orientation; the resourceful and practical me moves into motion. Now I am ready to do something with the people and situation in front of me—not just dream about different futures, clients, or organizations.

I'm reminded of a consultant who worked for me years ago. I sent him out to talk to some clients who had expressed a need. He came back saying that these clients were a real mess; they were not ready to deal with us yet, and we should wait until they were ready. In my view, this consultant was saying that the work begins there and then, not here and now. He was unwilling to jump into the fire with these clients; he wanted to wait for a better day.

To dream about alternative projects and better clients is to reject the real starting point. The idealistic me likes to play in a fantasy world that does not have to face reality. I can concoct a world of perfect clients and perfect organizations working with me, of course, the perfect consultant. But perfect clients in a perfect world do not need perfect consultants. Poof! and back to reality: these clients with their warts and wants, problems and possibilities. Jump in and embrace the work as it comes to you.

Simple Works

Imagine that you are a change consultant, living up to your label, consulting to an organization of three thousand people with six levels of hierarchy in five major divisions across four states selling three products that did not exist two years ago. How do you talk with, work with—change—this organization and its people? Messages full of subtlety are doomed. E-mails containing twenty-three action points will be lost. Well-intentioned executive speeches will evaporate into the air. Try simple. Simple works. Whether you are working with an organization of three thousand or a board meeting of twenty or a task team of six, when you are creating change, simple works. This is not good news to those of us who love our twelve-box models and our three-page systems flow charts. If you want to share your research with the organization, forget it. If you want to communicate subtlety, drop the idea. If you think eloquence will persuade them, better think again. As useful as those ideas might be at a professional meeting or a cocktail party, they need to be put aside in favor of what works. And what works? Simple, as in 1-2-3.

Bringing about change in a company of the size, depth, width, geography, and history I just described requires exceptional clarity. How many changes can three thousand people absorb together, at the same time? When there are six levels of hierarchy, how many actions can they own and take together? When the organization is spread across five divisions and four states, only a few core change messages can be carried effectively.

Search out the profoundly simple approach. Seek ways of presenting your message in an uncluttered fashion. Do clients the service of helping them distill their communications down to the most essential points. Distill required actions down to their most fundamental elements. Find the core of what you want and communicate that. Remove the tail fins, hubcaps, fender skirts, and sun visor; strip your message down to its essentials, allowing the nobility of the core design to show through. Unclutter your approach to the work.

Ask yourself, What one thing do they want to do together? If you don't know, find out. If they don't know, help them realize it. Or you might ask, What would you have them do right now? If you don't know, figure it out. If they don't know, tell them. Or ask, What unites them? Ask yourself. Ask them. Simple questions can cut through complexity. A few questions can unify people as they search for their answers in common. You are often called because of the complexity the client faces. For you to go in and make it even more complex is not a service.

I worry that I am simplifying because I am not smart enough to handle the confusion. That is a real possibility. On the other hand, I know that if I, a reasonably smart person, cannot understand, then many others probably cannot understand either. When I check, I find that this is true; my intuition is supported by experience. This encourages me to continue my search for simple expression and simple action.

Get Out of the Way

Getting out of the way means letting clients run their own organizations. It means continuing to be a consultant, not a manager. It means celebrating their accomplishments. It means keeping your mouth shut while they learn. It means helping them learn rather than doing their work. It requires patience, humility, and self-confidence.

I often get in the way. In the process of helping people in the organization do their work better, I can inadvertently allow my need for recognition to become a barrier to my effectiveness and their progress. My demonstrations of skill, wisdom, creativity, cleverness, and humor divert us from the task at hand. In retrospect, I can see many situations in which I was trying to get attention rather than trying to help. I was worried that they would not see my importance to what they were doing, or I was scared they would find out that they didn't need me.

Pursuing personal credit is especially detrimental to consultants. We are already in the favored, special position of having been called in to help the organization. People look to us for guidance and give us uncommon power. An exaggerated need for recognition and credit on our part can compound the problem of clients' dependence on us. We can end up taking on decision-making roles and responsibilities that really belong to the clients—all because personal needs pushed us into doing their job.

There is no easy answer for us needy consultants. Getting out of the way deprives us of attention from others; what can we substitute for that recognition from the clients? Briefly, recognition from ourselves. When we measure ourselves against our own standards, we can reward ourselves for what we have done. This is a bit of a test of our independence. We need to learn the rewards that come from watching others in action, knowing that we helped. I do get a great kick out of watching and helping people learn to deal with their work in more effective ways. I do feel great satisfaction when people I have worked with see their work from a life perspective. I love to hear about clients helping others in ways that I helped them. This subtle side of consulting is increasingly rewarding to me, but I have had to work at making it rewarding. I know it serves both me and the clients; I know that my personal needs are less likely to clutter the clients' work. And I still feel some frustration as I stand aside to let others do the work. Consider your motive for what you are doing with the clients: Is it centered on accomplishment for the organization or attention for yourself? Is your motive directed outward or inward?

Change Hurts

Change is more than uncomfortable, difficult, and irritating. None of those words captures the depth of the change experience. The word *hurt* is often used in association with harm and damage and pain, all negative words. Although change can indeed be harmful and damaging to the organization and the people in it, that is not the kind of change or hurt I am referring to. I believe that positive, healthy change usually hurts. It hurts the way your muscles hurt when you ask them to do something they are not used to doing; it hurts the way it does when your child has less time for you or when you must deal with aging parents. Change does not always hurt, but if it comes quickly and is important, it does. Gradual change over years rather than weeks will hurt less noticeably, but the hurt is not gone, just spread out. The changes you and I facilitate usually happen in a short time and therefore hurt more.

Even when individuals are choosing to change, the hurt is not eliminated. Changes that feel good to some people are often torturing others. Know that the change you represent is likely to hurt people. Do not dismiss their anxiety or withhold information from them. Help them choose the change and face the fear. Deal with them empathically. Acting as if all will be sweetness and light after a change is to neglect the reality of change and the impact on people. Allow for the hurt that comes with change and build care into your change processes. We who thrive on change—at least thrive on helping others change—might forget what it is like to be on the receiving end of our fine work.

Risk as You Expect Clients to Risk

Think of a client with whom you have dealt recently—someone with a major opportunity to move forward, an opportunity that requires significant risk. The potential gains are large, but imagine how the client sees this risky opportunity. Imagine how much risk that client faces. Now, are you willing to risk as much to help that client? Will you put yourself on the line to the same extent the client does?

We often hang on to our own perspective on risk and lose the client's perspective. This is analogous to watching someone build up the nerve to leap a five-foot chasm. If we have made the leap frequently and have guided many others in safe leaps, five feet is not much of a risk for us. But this person is on the edge right now, facing a new situation loaded with risk for him. See it from his perspective. What would be a similar test for us? How about an eight-foot gap? No? Then let's say it's a ten-foot chasm. Knowing that our own risk level is at ten feet, what kind of support would we like in order to attempt such a leap? That is the level of support we should bring to the person attempting five feet.

A person who is not used to confronting her boss may find it to be extremely difficult. I am used to doing it, and so are you. We have been confronting bosses for years. What is really hard for us may be confronting ourselves. We should bring to the person confronting her boss the kind of support we would like to have as we confront ourselves. Providing support to someone who is risking is a critical part of our work. I think we are too often oblivious to the risks being taken, effectively discouraging the risk taker. We act as though the risk being taken were not a risk, but normal. This attitude discourages the person taking the risk from acknowledging what she is going through, depriving her of the support we could offer.

Often clients hire me to do something that I have successfully done before—in fact, they do not want me to risk. I am their insurance as they risk doing something that is new for them. One way in which I judge how much I am risking is by the success of the projects I work on. A strong pattern of success, say 95 percent, can suggest that I have room to take much more risk than I am taking. Success might seem a silly thing to be concerned about, but in relation to risk, growth, and creativity, overwhelming success may be a negative indicator. If your work "always works" for you, then take a look at how much you are risking and how much you are learning.

Create Context

One of the main things I do for my clients is to build new context. I help people be themselves, but in different surroundings. What surrounds them is different from what it was a moment ago, allowing them to come up with new perspectives, insights, and decisions. They use the same knowledge, skills, and abilities they use each day, but in a different context. In effect, they become consultants to themselves.

How do I change context? One example: when you open this book, you step into my context, different from your own. As you read, you are seeing what you already know in relation to what I know.

Another example: I was helping six sales managers redefine their jobs. I asked each of them to think of the most important contributions a sales manager could make and to write down in bold lettering on separate sheets each of these potential contributions. Then I asked them to spread these pages on the floor around them for all to see. Last of all, I had them read, sort, and discuss their work, looking for patterns and discussing the importance of the contributions. All these steps created a new context in which they could think and work.

One more example: when a group of thirty supervisors was troubled about the motivation of their employees, I sent them out in pairs to meet with groups of employees and to ask those groups what motivates them. The pairs came back with all this information, which they posted for all thirty supervisors to see. As they read the postings, they were in a new context, bringing up new observations and new questions, opening themselves to new thought and action.

Shift context by considering the questions and information it would be useful for clients to be immersed in. Engage them in considering the possibilities, help them create the new setting, and ask them to step into it. In the three examples I have given here, readers stepped into my ideas, sales managers surrounded themselves with their own ideas, and supervisors surrounded themselves with employees' ideas. These surroundings caused people to think and work differently than they had in the past. To put it simply, creating context is about taking the same old people and having them work with information and each other in new ways.

Seed Hope

I bring clients hope. They need to believe, "We want to do something about this, and we can!" and I help them believe it. If clients are without hope, all planned actions will likely remain just plans. Hope comes when new perspectives generate new alternatives. Clients often call when they have already tried everything. They feel stuck, if not hopelessly stuck. Suggestions of actions within their old perspective usually result in such responses as, "We've already tried that," "That won't work because . . .," "They won't let us do that," "We can't do that here." At this point, I usually begin to feel pretty hopeless, too. I get stuck along with them, feeling that maybe it is not possible to do anything.

Just before I despair, my bias toward hopefulness saves me! I begin to look at the organization through new eyes, toward the possibilities. I then help people get their minds off their present problems and focus on the future they would like to create together. In the process of envisioning the possible future, people regenerate hope. Hope comes from their common vision of what they want added to the belief that they can do something about it. Seeding an organization with hope involves helping people first understand the difference between what they have and what they want and then see that they can do something to close the gap. As people take responsibility, as they act together, and as they see old problems in new ways, they grow hopeful. The hope they grow then seeds new efforts, new actions, and even more hope.

Seeding hope does not mean putting aside all those things that are wrong, unjust, broken, unfair, mistaken, crazy, out of whack, or otherwise messed up. In fact, hope often involves facing into all of this mess. People can continue to gripe about the problems they have, or the stupidity of the system, or the management's style. All that griping doesn't accomplish much, and it means less when put into perspective with the hope and possibilities that have been generated. In fact, many of the daily problems that people have been complaining about but unwilling to act on finally begin to get real attention.

There are hopeless situations that deserve to be abandoned. When the chances of improvement are so small that they do not deserve people's investment, do not invest. Find something more constructive to do. Seeding hope when it is truly hopeless is irresponsible.

Persevere

I am in this work for the long haul, and I am working with this client for the long haul. I recall a plant manager telling his staff, "Deal with Geoff as though he were going to be here for years. See him as a resource available to you whenever you need him. He is not here to work on a single project, but on long-term change." That perspective had a profound effect on our work. It reduced my impatience and required my perseverance. My actions in that plant were positively different because of my client's long-term commitment and mine.

Effective organizational change is not accomplished through a series of one-night consulting stands. Effective consultation requires us to build a relationship for the long term, as in a marriage. We and our clients invest in more than just the present event; we see this event as part of what has happened and what will happen. By hanging in there for the long term, we gain a deep knowledge of how the organization moves and breathes. Such knowledge results in interventions that are attuned to how the organization actually lives, rather than to how we imagine it works. Gaining this deeper knowledge requires that we work through the less glorious, less momentous times. It is patience-testing, commitment-testing work that can produce growth.

Choosing to pursue this long-term relationship assures me of some hard times as I help clients struggle with their issues. For my "troubles," I will learn about the organization in depth; I will learn its culture, rituals, norms, systems, and people. I will be called on to help with opportunities and problems I have not faced before. I will not always be helpful; sometimes my work will get in the way. I will risk and learn in the process.

Find the Client in Yourself

From one perspective, all the work I do, I do within myself. All my work with clients, I have to complete within myself. I am effective with clients to the extent that I can make them part of me. Somehow, I must become them or find them in a part of myself. So, because it all happens "in here," all my work with clients is work with parts of me.

To a great extent, my success in fully understanding clients depends on having had experiences like the ones they are having. When clients tell me that I understand them at an intellectual, emotional, physical, and spiritual level, I know I have found the client within myself. When I can demonstrate their thoughts or feelings to them, when I can accurately interpret how they might handle a situation, then I know I am ready to help. I "become" the client; I "am" the problem, the dilemma, the opportunity, the contradiction—whatever it is that the client brought to me.

Here is an example that has come up in some form at least fifty times. Picture me working with a group of people who are very reactive to the larger organization they are part of, who are angry about being "put in this position." According to them, management only tells them when they do things wrong and never tells them what they are supposed to do. Furthermore, they cannot change things because no one listens to them. In addition, they do not get the respect in the organization they deserve. They probably ought to report to a higher level, too. This is all said with some petulant anger, even a whining tone. If you have consulted to more than ten groups, I am sure you have run into this type.

While they are talking, I search for similar experiences in myself—and I do not have to search very hard. Their complaints sound very much like some I voiced when I was an employee. I do not have to imagine much to identify with this group. I also notice the anger I have at management and at an organization that doesn't respect or use me as I'd like to be used. I feel abused, unappreciated, unheard, not respected, and angry! I tell the group this with some passion. And they let me know that I understand them.

We are all in the same sinking boat! I search deeper within my angry, abused self and find something that initially

I didn't notice: I am angry at others, but I am also angry at myself for putting up with all this garbage! I have chosen this job, I have chosen to accept its garbage, I have chosen to be quiet (until now), and I have chosen to be a victim! Recognizing my responsibility, my part in the problem, is a first step to getting out of this mess I am in. And helping the client group do the same is often the first step for them.

My advantage as their consultant is that I chose to be here with them temporarily, and I have experience with coming in and getting out. By finding the client inside myself, I can find alternative paths that help the clients outside myself. This approach works in many ways. The clients know that I understand very well what is going on with them; they can see my acceptance of them and their situation. They hear me talking about having related experiences and they hear me laughing at myself, sometimes even at my own stupidity or mistakes or weakness. My understanding helps them open to considering alternative actions or changes they might make to get out of the fix they are in.

You Are Your Best Intervention

The techniques I use, the designs I create, and the recommendations I put forth are all potentially useful. The new ways of thinking, the alternative perspectives, the new context—these are all valuable. But they often pale by comparison to presence, to being there. Check this against your own experience. When I am in the room, clients hold a better meeting than when I am not—even if I don't do anything. Clients behave differently because I am there, not just because of what I do. Clients reinforce this observation when they say, "That was really a good meeting today; thanks for your help," "That session would have gone a lot differently if you hadn't been there," or "Thanks to you, we are really making progress!" The striking thing about each of these comments is that they were said following meetings in which I did very little.

It is as if we consultants become minor totems. We stand for what the organization strives for; therefore, the people invested in this striving behave differently around us. Or perhaps our presence puts people on their best behavior, as they are when company comes or when they are in the presence of a person "of the cloth." A related story: a client told me about a series of decisions she had managed particularly well and was very proud of. She attributed much of her success to her work with me because during the process she would ask herself, "What would Geoff suggest that I do?" She described all that I would have suggested and how she followed these "suggestions" successfully. I listened, impressed with the innovative steps she had taken, and congratulated her on her accomplishment. I also told her that what she had done was much more effective and creative than what I probably would have recommended. This amazed her; she thought she was doing just what I would have recommended. I understand what she did, because I have used other consultants in the same way. Their phantom presence has guided me.

Early in this chapter, I suggested that you use my wisdom about change to create your own. Reflect on what I've said and your experience; list a dozen or so guides you use when working with changing organizations. This is a good way to remind yourself of what you have learned while doing your consulting work.

Twenty

How *Not* to
Create Change

xperience has taught me much about what works but also about what does not work. Each project tells me something; sometimes I learn. Every project is a mix of what works and what does not. There is no such thing as having everything work well on a major change project. I have difficulty learning from my failures because I go to such great lengths to avoid acknowledging them. But over the years, I have learned something even there.

The very nature of change tells you that you are going to be walking in territory where the client has not previously set foot. All your plans and preparation, though essential, are best guesses about what will happen. As you would for any expedition, you need to prepare yourself and your client for the unexpected. Then when it happens, all of you will be saying, "We expected something like that." But you will not anticipate everything. You will be unpleasantly surprised. This chapter stands on the foundation of the mistakes I have made more than once. I hope to speed up your learning by sharing them with you.

There are too few resources. We enter the project with naive expectations about how much time, money, material, equipment, and energy this will take. It always requires at least twice as much as we imagined and got approval for in the first place. This often causes key decision makers to pull back just when we need more resources.

There is too much training. The change project requires that people learn new terminology, systems, roles, or skills. Much time and money is poured into giving people what they need to make the change work—so much time and money that the training itself begins to be seen as the focus of the project, when it actually is just a supporting piece. Everyone acts as if this place will change when we have all had the training. That seldom happens; the support needed back on the job is usually much more important than the training, and if it is not there, the project fails.

There is a lack of leadership. Those parties that signed on to support the effort from beginning to infinity were around for the kickoff and now cannot be found. Leadership requires vision, not just authority. Leadership means having the bigger picture, knowing what the pieces are and how all the pieces could fit together. It means consistent, persistent pursuit of the change vision. Change priorities become part of organizational priorities; people and mechanisms are put in place to see that change happens. Too often, at the very time the project needs clear leadership, the leaders are absent; they have moved off to their latest priority. Yes, management is among these likely culprits, but so are many of the rest of us—including the consultant, for example: Where are we two years after we help get this started?

Change is pursued as an event. Change events are large, focal meetings during which change is talked about and resolutions are made, yet little happens afterwards . . . until the next change event. There is no apparent connection between the events; there is no larger plan or design. There is regular resolve to do something differently around here—all too similar to a semiannual resolution to lose weight that lasts for a week or two.

Change is pursued in isolation. People involved in change seal themselves off from the rest of the organization. This allows them to focus, to concentrate their energies, to produce, and to escape the complexity of day-to-day organization living. It also allows them to lose touch, to become the anointed elite, to see the organization through narrow models, to fail to keep up on what is really going on, to create a gap between themselves and everyone else. All this in the pursuit of good change.

There is "flavor of the year" change. Not flavor of the week or month, but of the year. This is the top-down effort to shake the foundations of the organization. Everyone is involved, and the slogan on the banners uses words like *commitment, quality, team, scorecard, number one,* or *best.* We give it one really good push to get it running down through the organization, and it runs out of gas long before it begins to positively affect performance. After a year of rest, there's a new flavor, and here we go again!

There are many unconnected changes. Projects and programs are pursued as if they had nothing to do with each other—even though many of the same people may be involved in these various efforts. Once a client and I totaled up the organization-wide change projects under way in that one telecommunications company: thirty-seven! A graphic portrayal of all of these projects looks like a plate of spaghetti, they are so intertwined and connected and twisted about each other. But day-to-day pursuit of each project does not acknowledge these twists and turns; each project is led with little regard for all the others happening around it. The projects compete with each other for time, money, and people.

Meaning is lost in methods. In the frenzy of finding good tools and methods, practical folks in organizations often lose the meaning and purpose that the tools were designed to support. Application zealots lockstep their way through total quality or balanced scorecard or appreciative inquiry. They lose sight of the larger meaning of the models they are following. They get caught up in the How and lose the Why. You may have heard, "Just tell us how to do this; don't bother with the philosophy," or "Theory is fine, but what are the basic steps that will get us there?" In this country, maybe this hemisphere, we have a fascination with *doing* that allows us to skip conceptualizing and planning. We miss out on meaning as we jump into methods. In the process, we lose the ability to think for ourselves.

Pursuit of deep meaning is not honored in most large organizations—especially corporations, with their built-in dollar incentive. Whether we are talking about the deeper meaning of this company, this product, or this individual, pursuit of meaning finds itself at odds with pursuit of profit. What readily unites us around a company are the numbers and profits, which represent company and personal success. We find it easy to talk with others at this dollar-oriented level. Discussing meaning and purpose and aspiration is another matter. To do that, we have to reach deeper than into our pocketbooks; we have to reach into ourselves and decide how much we want to reveal. And the rules about expressing meaning are not as clear as they are around money. Meaning is personal, and we know by working around others that we assign different meanings to the work we do. We usually do not talk about why; we talk about what and how, when and where. Our organizational cultures dictate against grasping the meaning behind the methods in change projects—even though the meaning is essential to success.

Part Six

The Marketplace

Twenty-One

You and the Marketplace

As you may have detected, making money in the marketplace is not my primary reason for being a consultant. We serve our larger purpose in the marketplace, and we also serve the marketplace—in that order, when all is going well. It's an *immense* marketplace and one that doesn't care very much about you or me. It's not against us; it's not trying to punish us; it's not trying to get us or get even; it's not for us and trying to reward us. The marketplace simply does not care. We care, and we care a lot! We step out the door, onto the Internet, or into a meeting, and bring our business and our selves with us. We step into a swirl of activity that is far beyond our understanding or even influence. Oh sure, we can act on what is before us, but there are large, uncontrollable forces that sweep through the market and our lives—for better and for worse. When the market winds blow our small craft in a favorable direction, carrying us swiftly and successfully forward, we get excited and often a bit inflated in the process. We are inclined to take too

195

much credit for what happened; we think the market gods favor us. When the winds blow against us, capsizing our small craft, we often take that personally too. We are inclined to take too much blame for what happened, and we think the gods are against us. But in reality, most of what is happening comes from the dynamics of the immense and immeasurable market beast that does not care one whit whom or what it is hurling about. And we are caught up in its effects and make up our stories.

Perhaps I should have written "I" rather than "we" throughout that opening paragraph; I can see my patterns. But I also see these same patterns in other consultants and my clients. The marketplace calls for humility, not domination. As long as you are a part of it, you will be learning about it—or you had better be! Its power, vastness, and mystery are also its fascination. Whether you are trying to comprehend an emerging industry, a new political administration, or the vagaries of your favorite client, the marketplace is always intriguing. When it quits being intriguing, get out.

The two preceding paragraphs set the tone for what I offer here. Lean toward the mysteries of the marketplace rather than away from them; learn from this real world where you make a living and a life. That's one lesson I've learned.

Since the publication of the first edition of this book, I myself have learned much more about marketing and the marketplace. I can now make my main points in one chapter rather than three, leaving more expert marketers to give you their guidance. In particular, look at books by Alan Weiss of Summit Consulting (his website is listed in the Resources). He has useful, pragmatic advice you will find helpful, and he approaches the market with more zeal for engagement than I can muster. I will draw from my experience those ideas that have helped me risk and helped me survive in the tougher times. This chapter contains some how-to guidance, but much of it is from a "why-to" perspective.

In the marketplace, you are successful if you have clients who pay you. Marvin Weisbord told me that years ago, before I went into consulting. It's not about how much you know or how you dress or how helpful you are or what your website looks like; it's about an exchange of consulting services for money. Pretty crass—and pretty true; that's how the marketplace decides if you are succeeding. Your challenge is to create your own more compelling definition of success, one that probably includes market considerations but is not dominated by them. That's what making your way in the marketplace is all about.

Fear of Selling Ourselves

"I really like the work, but I can't imagine making cold calls." "Selling myself to people I don't know is really repugnant to me." "How can I face a potential client when hardly anyone else is using me and I need the money!" To enter the marketplace as a buyer presents no problem; but when we are vendors and what we are vending is our talent and ourselves, then it's another matter. We look around disdainfully at other vendors selling used cars, aluminum siding, carpet cleaning, roach control, and love, and we hesitate to put ourselves among them. To say this differently, we are afraid to put ourselves out there. If it weren't for this fear, the world would be neck-deep in consultants! Competition and the marketplace keep many people out of this work. Marketing and selling your consulting services can be a much richer experience than standing on the curb throwing kisses to passersby. The marketplace is not an easy place for the fainthearted, but great rewards are possible in facing its challenges.

I have often attempted to sell my services to clients, usually after they've said they want the work done and I know I'm a strong contender. But my sales techniques have not been very effective. When I begin to sell my services to clients, I get uneasy. I feel presumptuous: How do I know they need me? At the same time, I am quite comfortable helping potential clients look at their needs and explaining what I have done that may fit. I want clients to choose to call me because they need my resources, not because I need theirs. I work at allowing the opportunity to happen.

Create Coincidence

How do I market myself well enough that I do not have to sell? To say it another way: What can I do today that encourages people to contact me tomorrow? And yet another way: How do I create a life that automatically yields the rewards I seek? Three versions of the same question, each from a different angle. I much prefer people calling me to my calling them. I am less skillful and comfortable at initiating sales contacts. I want to play to my strengths. In the market, you will not see me out on the street buttonholing people and enticing them to work with me; you will find me sitting in my office at home, waiting for people to call, write, or show up.

And why would they do this? Because they have heard of me somewhere else—usually from at least two separate sources. They spoke to a client who used me and a person who likes me. Or they read an article and heard about a book I have written. Or they talked to me once years ago, and recently someone mentioned working with me. Those are the coincidences that I want to help create. Looking back over the last thirty years inside and outside organizations, I can see years during which I was unknowingly putting this little creative coincidence structure in place. I wish now that I'd known what I was doing! I could have done it more intentionally.

You can start doing it now. Consider all the ways that people can meet and experience you. No, it is not enough to "network" and pass out your card; others must get a taste of who you are and what you offer. When you meet people and discuss issues with them, they get a taste of you and your thinking. When you post a paper on a listserv, people get a more distant but nevertheless useful sense of what you know and how you can help them. Even better, if you write a series of short papers, you reinforce your identity in their minds. When people see that you are on a panel for the local professional society and then meet you, these two "hits" on you mean much more than either one alone. The more you do out there in the marketplace, the more likely you will be creating coincidences.

This is not some strategy of the month; you need to think of it more as the intention of a lifetime. It requires everlasting patience. Why? Because you must take each action for the reward that is in the moment and not for the coincidence that might happen later. For example, give two hours to a person struggling with a work issue. Leave that discussion saying to yourself, "I really enjoyed working with her for two hours! And I think I was helpful. I hope we see each other again." Don't leave it thinking, "Bingo! There's a client! What do I do to reel her in? She really owes me now," or "That was a complete waste of time; she didn't say one thing about maybe hiring me to do some work." Nope, the meeting itself is the cake; if any work comes from it, that would be frosting.

Lay Tracks and Wait

My best marketing is supported by work I've already done for other people. My challenge is to find ways that will allow potential clients to know that I exist and am available to do similar good work for them. Given my inclinations, I will choose ways that do not intrude on these clients-to-be. I won't be out knocking on doors; as I said, I will be sitting in my office waiting. So I have had to learn to wait. I have found it a difficult skill to master, but over the years I've learned that the business world will serve up something I'm interested in doing if I'm patient enough. So far, I haven't been disappointed.

How long is the wait between my initial meeting with a potential client and the call exploring whether I might help her? Loooooooonnng! Far longer than I ever imagined when I started consulting. I thought that an expressed desire to work with me would shortly be followed by real work. Often four, six, eighteen months pass before something that looks like real work begins to happen. So I wait. While waiting, I do other things. I go to lunch with friends, mow the lawn, go to a movie, do work for other clients, read, or maybe go hiking. When in my best frame of mind, I look at this time as a gift. I continue to wait and remind myself to be patient. The patience part is important because its opposite produces anxiety in me, which family, clients, and potential clients pick up on. The anxiety ruins the time I have to do other things.

When We Need Work

When I need work . . . I mean, when I *neeeeeeed* work . . . my normally calm exterior develops a frantic edge. My mental and emotional wheels shift to a higher-pitched gear.

My ability to say no is bound, gagged, and thrown in a deserted back room of my mind. My head is compelled to nod yes and affirm everything a potential client says. My mind is partly on the work and mainly shouting, "House payments! Car payments! College tuition! Credit card payments! Food!" I smell the money and fixate on it. I notice the disconnect between what I am thinking about and what I am saying to the client.

Being "hungry" does not qualify me to do the work before me. It doesn't disqualify me either; it is simply not relevant to the client's needs. When that internal shouting is out of synch with the conversation with the client, I should be concerned. I'm pretending to be someone I'm not, and that is the path to dissatisfaction with myself and my work.

While I am going through my mental gyrations, what is the client doing? To begin with, many clients are suspicious of consultants—a well-founded suspicion, as I see it. They get even more suspicious if they think that this consultant in front of them—me—wants this work primarily for the money. Clients would prefer the consultant to be busy on twelve projects like theirs in other respected organizations. They want years of expertise backing the consultant's every move. They don't want the consultant to need the work or the money. So when they see dollar signs flashing in the consultant's eyes, they draw back. When they hear the consultant pushing to get the work without looking more deeply into it, they wonder. When the consultant agrees to a date without even looking at his calendar, that is worrisome. And afterward when a client sees the consultant out in the parking lot with his entire family leaping with joy around the car they all live in, this does not bring a similar joy to the client's heart! Yes, I exaggerate, but you get the point. Somehow I, you, must maintain a perspective that separates our more pressing needs from clients' needs. We will meet our needs by meeting theirs first, rather than the other way around.

Business Begets Business

Business comes from people who know me, and over years this group has expanded geometrically—as it likely will for you. Business begets business; clients beget clients. Each year of successful consulting broadens your potential client base. For example, many of the people with whom I had worked in the past continued to work with me as they moved from organization to organization. They moved and brought me along. Old business has always been my primary source of new business—one more reason to do an especially good job with today's clients.

Most of my consulting has been for large organizations with thousands of employees. One of the results is that they pass me around. What I did in this division is now asked for in another. The approach used in the Western Region is successful, so three other regions are interested. The clients do the marketing for me; they see to it that I get the calls. There were six large organizations that I worked with for between eight to fourteen years. That's a lot of selling I did not have to do.

I know there is a certain amount of "You can't get into the water until you know how to swim" in this advice. This just reinforces the point I've made elsewhere in this book about doing work wherever you can, for money or for none. Invest in building your experience now so you can capitalize on it later.

Twenty-Two

Making the Leap into Consulting

The "leap" is a great image to accompany the feelings that come with leaving safe, paid work you know how to do for the insecurity of the occasional pay that comes with the work you want to do. There you are in midair, having left the ground of the work you know, on your way to the work you want, momentarily held aloft by your strong push off, and gravity is taking over. That is what it felt like to me as I made the leap years ago.

The first edition this book attracted many people who were seriously thinking about becoming consultants or were brand-new to consulting or were just fantasizing about it. This chapter is especially for those kinds of readers. It is intended to help you decide whether you want to make the leap and how you might do it. It deals with the problems of leaving the regular payroll and joining the ranks of the occasionally employed, and like all the other chapters, it is based on my experience. I worked fourteen years inside organizations before cutting the corporate umbilical

203

cord. Many people ask me how I did it and how they can do it. I don't know the answers to all aspects of their questions, but I know enough to help you think about what you want to do.

Several years into my corporate career, I began thinking about whether I might want to be a consultant one day. Before I had even begun thinking about it, I had done some things that ended up being quite useful to me later as a consultant. I had unintentionally prepared myself to be an external consultant; you can be much more intentional right now if you have a job. Here is what I did and what you could do:

Join a professional support group	Lead public workshops	Do internal consulting
Speak to civic organizations	Attend public workshops	Present papers at conferences
	Publish articles	Meet consultants

I did all these things because I wanted to learn and contribute—or be recognized. These efforts each took my time and my employers' money, and they didn't make any money for me. If I'd known that I would be a consultant one day, I would have done each of these more intensely. I could have learned much more than I did.

The primary boost to my eventual launch as a consultant was the experience I gained working for three Fortune 500 companies. Much of the work I did there was closely related to what I do now. I loved the work and loved working for large organizations. This positive experience significantly affects how I work with clients. They can see that I love this work and respect them for what they are trying to do. They know I believe that people can find life's meaning through their work in corporations.

They do not see me as someone who hates corporations but is forced to leech off them to make a living. Quite the opposite. Compare that perspective with your own.

From early in my corporate career, I lacked the attraction to or passion for climbing the corporate ladder. That characteristic turned out to be a strong indicator of consulting potential. Work in an organization gave me a place to achieve, to contribute, to gain recognition, but I did not need to move upward to feel successful. I wanted to do interesting work and went after it, though not always in a politically wise fashion. I was able to involve myself with important work and clients without the distraction of wondering whether I would be an executive one day. I acted like an independent consultant even when I was a dependent consultant. The nature of the work, a love of the work, an achievement orientation, work with executives, and some management experience—all these serve me well now and have helped me define my uniqueness and usefulness with my clients. How would you define your own?

Start Building a Client Base

Building a client base can start years before your actual move to external consulting. You can certainly be much more intentional about it than I was. In addition to skills and experience, there are three facets to build: a list of potential clients, a stack of writings about your work, and a number of public presentations.

Build a list of potential clients. Keep track of the people you work with who are potential future clients. Recall my earlier guidance about where business comes from, namely, the people with whom you have worked. Especially note their movement to other companies and the positions they hold there. Collect addresses and phone numbers that you might use later; you will need them to track down your contacts. My first seven clients included five people with whom I had worked closely in the previous six years. If I had known that would be the case, I would have prepared better for it.

Like other people trying to make a sale, we will probably start with those who know us and our work best. Insurance salespeople start with relatives; we start with former associates, employers, and internal clients. And let's face it: if your former associates are not willing to hire you, why should complete strangers be interested? You need a very good answer to that question. I recall getting a call from a former coworker, who was now a vice president of a West Coast company. He had heard I was on my own, and he wanted to work with me again. I asked, "On what?" He replied, "Don't worry about that, just come on out; we'll figure something out." That's welcome validation early in a consultant's new practice!

Build a portfolio of writing. Start writing now, and if you can, start publishing now. Ten years before I became a consultant, I began writing an article a year. It turned out that years later those articles were of value to me as a consultant. Some of them served as literature for clients and as handouts for training sessions. All of them served to distinguish me a bit from that large crowd of consultants from whom potential clients have to choose. These articles even gave me a little name recognition in a few places. Write to your potential clients about work you have done or want to do. Don't wait; start writing now and get your articles out for others to see. Publish in the wider press if you can, but do not worry if you cannot. With today's technology you can write and publish an article on your own or on the Internet.

Build your presentation experience. Many organizations search for presenters at their weekly or monthly meetings. They are less interested in consultants who might see their organization as a selling platform. While you are still inside an organization, you are less likely to be seen as someone selling to your personal advantage. Talk with professional groups in your city about what you are doing in your organization. In the process, people get to know you. Offer to train people in subjects that are of interest to you, subjects that will eventually be part of your consulting repertoire. Many national conferences are looking for presenters who want to share their companies' experiences.

On Being a Lone Consultant

The most important differences between being an internal consultant and an external consultant are not related to skills. You need similar skills in both positions. What is different? First, you will notice the absence of regular paychecks, an expense account, health benefits, sick leave, and a retirement plan. And you will notice there is no one to sort your mail, make photocopies, answer the phone, and buy paper or paper clips. No one trains you, tells you what the policy is, keeps you up-to-date on where the organization is going, introduces you to team members, or trades gossip with you. No one finds work for you to do, assumes that you ought to be involved, or expects you to be around in two years.

There are many resources at your disposal on the inside that just flat disappear when you go outside. The further up the hierarchy you are now, the more you will notice the resource gap when you leave. All this affects your motivation and tests your skills. Unhooking from your organizational life-support systems has implications for your personal power and energy. Your expectations of consulting will be tested against the reality of it. And enough of your expectations must be met to more than counterbalance the negatives you are sure to experience. When you ask yourself what you expect to get out of being an external consultant, your best answers come from your heart and not from your head. You must have the heart to support the loss of organizational support, security, salary, and infrastructure. External consultants have to go inside themselves to find the motivation to survive alone in the world.

Silence and Dependence

Choosing to be an independent external consultant means choosing to be alone. Not all of the time, but certainly much more than our counterparts in corporate life or even those in consulting firms. Getting comfortable with being alone is critical to thriving as a consultant on your own. I am reminded of divorce: two people who have spent years together choose to live apart. One of the first things each must learn is how to live alone, how to be responsible for his or her own life without being in a relationship with another person. Leaving the world of large organizations and setting up shop in a spare room is similar to divorce. From the beginning, I noticed how quiet it was, that the phone seldom rang, that there was no one to have coffee with, that I had to decide what to do next, that there were no other offices to wander to, that I had no associates to chat with. I could show up naked! Nobody cared! I did not feel nearly as important as I had a few days earlier back in the organization.

Fourteen years in organizations slowly blinded me to my dependence on their people, systems, structure, and culture. So much of what I did was in relation to, in support of, this organization, and that gave me meaning. I was surprised to discover this dependence; I really thought I was more self-determined than that. There's an old story that seems related. A couple lives right next to the railroad tracks in the city. Every morning at 3:37, every morning for years, an express train roars past their bedroom window. This morning at 3:37, there is no train, no roar. When the train does not go by, they both awaken suddenly, frightened out of their sleep, exclaiming, "What was that!?" "That" in my case was the absence of the organization; it did not arrive on schedule at the beginning of my day as it had for fourteen years. The silence was deafening and frightening.

We are not condemned to isolation. There are alternatives: joining a consulting firm, forming a consortium, building a professional support group. We can find ways to meet some of the needs that were met in the organization. The complication is that we must also make a living. When I worked in an organization, spending most of an afternoon chatting around in the offices had little evident impact on my paychecks. Opportunities to earn were not necessarily lost. Doing the same thing as an independent—and doing it regularly—can be costly.

Need for Nurture

When your needs for nurture push aside your pursuit of business, notice. When you are lonely and find yourself seeking out relationships like those you had back in the organization and delaying making contact in the market-place, watch out. If this becomes a pattern, consider whether you really do want to have your own one-person business. Some of my consultant friends have chosen to join larger firms, to take partners, or to go back into orga-nization life because of this need to be affiliated with oth-ers. Some of these consultants were doing quite well financially, but their "people" needs were not being met. Others were not doing as well financially; their need for comrades blocked their motivation to find work.

Though I love working with other people, I don't need to be with them all the time. My more introverted side is supported by the time alone that consulting gives me. What do I do to take care of my need for contact with other people? My telephone bills and e-mail exchanges reveal that I stay in regular contact with friends and asso-ciates across the country. I belong to a professional devel-opment and support group that meets quarterly and has for twenty-five years. And of course, I have a few local friends that I see on a regular basis.

As in the case of a divorce, it takes some time to adjust to and learn about being alone at work. After the ini-tial exhilaration of starting the business wears off, after hav-ing told everyone twenty times how exciting it is to do this, after designing the letterhead and business card—after all that, you come face to face with . . . yourself. There is no one else there. What are you going to do now? Not having done this before and coming from a long relationship you could count on, you will be uncertain and awkward. And why not? Why should you be good at this? The awkward-ness and uncertainty are filled with potential and excite-ment. One of the best reasons to become an independent consultant is to learn about yourself, and that opportunity it does not provide the psychological glue an association or affiliation needs.

If you are new to consulting and do not have much business, you may want to contact other consultants about the possibility of working for them as a subcontractor. Subcontractors do work that the contractors do not have the time, expertise, or inclination to do. As a subcontractor, you provide services needed in return for money. Contractors make their money on the difference between what they bill the client and what they pay you.

What are the primary considerations involved in this arrangement? You are in effect paying the contractor to do the marketing and find work for you. On a long project, this could be worth it. Of course, the work you do is limited to what the contractor finds. Many subcontractors struggle with the fact that they are billed out at a rate that is much higher than what they are paid. They wonder why they should have to accept this lower rate for work the client is obviously willing to pay more for. In this, their struggle is the same as that of the consultant employed in a large firm. Many resolve this dilemma by seeking their own work; others see the advantages of not having to search for work and not having to be totally responsible.

Work Solo or as a Firm Manager?

Though I have chosen to work alone in my practice, I have toyed with the idea of having others in this little firm with me. Here is my recurring internal debate: when it is just me, I do not have to check with anyone at work on what I decide to do. If I were the manager of my own firm, I would have others to talk to about my work and where the firm is going. Working alone, I can work part-time, full-

greets you very quickly—though it may be costu
ways that alarm you more than encourage you.

Independent? Associate? Partner? Subcontracto

I see at least four reasons to associate yourself with oth
ers in a firm rather than be on your own: (1) persona
inclination—you like working with others more than
being alone; (2) marketing—as we discussed earlier, you
have major discomfort with marketing and selling yourself;
(3) business—you don't have any and others do; (4) abilities—
your current skills are too narrow to stand on their own in
the marketplace, you could build new skills by being part
of a firm, or both.

Most people associate themselves with a firm for one
of the last two reasons. Many see it as an interim step to
being completely on their own. As a result, consulting
firms are busily engaged in training their associates to be
the eventual competition. The contracts signed on entering
a firm are getting more and more complicated as firms try
to protect their business from departing associates. Let that
serve as a caution for those of you who plan to use someone else's business as a stepping-stone for your own.

Some consultants have been successful working
together in something less than a firm, a kind of loose affiliation of professionals. They refer business to each other.
On a project-by-project basis, they decide on financial
arrangements. They support their loose structure because
they want to continue to work with each other. An affiliation based on mutual needs and skills will likely hold
together better than one based primarily on financial considerations. Why? Because though money attracts people,

time, or double-time and not involve others in deciding. If I have even one person working for me full-time, my job moves toward being full-time too. I would feel a full-time responsibility for that one person. As long as I am working by myself, I can work out of my home. When I add one person, or five, this quickly becomes impossible, and I have to rent an office, buy more furniture, and commute to my office—probably in a suit instead of my pajamas.

There is more. Working by myself, I only get paid when I am working. If I had a person working for me, I would make money when that person worked. And if I had five people, I could make five times as much. If I ran a small firm of six to eight people, we could take on projects much larger than any I can consider now all by myself. We could learn more and earn more. As the owner of a consulting business that builds a positive reputation over the years, perhaps with a small line of products as well as consulting services, I could build equity that others would be willing to pay for. I could sell the firm and make a million . . . maybe. As a one-person operation, everything I do involves me. I don't have much to sell to anyone else, should I decide to retire. There is no equity to put on the market. A firm with a few consultants requires full-time support staff and the related equipment: computers, copy machines, fax machines, printers, and so on. There is great advantage to having this human and electronic help close at hand. As an individual working alone, I find myself licking stamps, making copies, typing reports, collating pages, paying bills, and performing many other activities that do not use my best talents.

I have talked with many consultants who have struggled to build a firm from a solo practice. It seems to require at least eight consultants to give the firm's owner the flexibility he or she had as an individual working alone.

Four- to six-person firms seem to be surviving more often than thriving; they are at a critical in-between point in their growth. Eight productive consultants begin to justify the overhead of an office manager to take some of the burden that the owner has been carrying. It also is at about this point that the owner can begin to profit financially from all the work being done by his or her consultants.

Preparing for This Work

A paper I wrote in the third grade began, "When I grow up, I want to be a bartender." That is as close as I came to putting myself on the consulting path at an early age. (Actually, when I wrote that paper, I think most consultants *were* bartenders! There is a kinship between the two professions.) Most of us grow into consulting out of related work. My experience biases me in that direction. I have no formal academic preparation to do the work I am doing. And I see many consultants who have built successfully on previous life and work experience, without having strong academic credentials. Most of them didn't plan to be consultants when they started working. I suspect they are better consultants for the diverse experiences they have had.

Now we are seeing a crop of mature, savvy consultants who did their graduate work years ago and supplemented it with work inside organizations before going out on their own. Some became consultants too early for my taste; I think they should have spent years in organizations before consulting to them. There is no substitute for that inside perspective. And it builds credibility with clients too. One of the best ways of preparing to help others in their work is to do that work ourselves for a while. The consultant's role is a step removed from the work. To take that step too early can preclude a deeper understanding of what the work is about. When I hear about a manager of ten years making time to pursue an advanced degree, that excites me. The person is adding education to his or her substantial life and work experience, to the benefit of the individual and of future clients.

These are just a few of the considerations involved in making the leap to external consulting. Supplement this chapter by interviewing other experienced consultants. All of us together can help you make your best choice.

Twenty-Three

Stepping Back from Consulting

One profound shift has taken place in my life since the publication of the first edition of this book: I have taken a large step back from the regular world of work. For the last five years, I have been working only four to eight paid days a year, days when my clients still see me as a consultant, though most of them are aware of the shift I have made. This chapter is about this shift, not because you are currently anticipating doing the same thing, but because someday you will be. The chapter begins with a brief description of what has happened to me over the last five years; that background introduces what I have learned. You may be interested in the story itself, but it is the learning gained from living the story that is most important.

The Story

It has always been my expectation that I would ply my consulting wares until I was at least seventy years old. Fewer paid days by that time, but at least thirty a year. It hasn't turned out that way. Though I have always worked less than most people, I never consciously intended to stop. Then, five years ago, Sheila and I were meeting with our financial adviser. He told us that if we lived within some financial boundaries, we could quit working for money starting that day. I had never seriously considered such a possibility. To hear him express it as a reality was unsettling; I felt anxious and disoriented. In fact, if we had been required to evacuate the building at that moment, they would have had to carry me out! I could not have stood up and walked, I was that shocked. He had torn up my mental maps of my life; I lacked the ability and confidence to move. An hour later, I was able to walk but still in a daze of disbelief and discomfort. It was weeks before I began to accept the reality of this new life stage. Leaving the world of regular work was not initially an attractive prospect for me. I did do it; I now celebrate my new place in the community, but I did not start out feeling very celebratory.

I think I have chosen to move to this stage of my life for reasons similar to those that brought me to consulting in the first place: it was time to do something new, to contribute in a new way, to discover more of myself. As wonderful as the role of corporate consultant had been for me, I knew that I wanted to do something different. When told I could afford to try, I decided to, and it was the not-for-profit (NFP) community that gradually became more and more attractive to me. It has become the place I apply many of the skills I learned in the for-profit world—with some twists, as we will discuss later.

Clarity about my new role has come gradually; it started before I was aware of it, years before I stepped back from corporate consulting. I had been giving time outside my paid work for years, as I mentioned early in this book. Right now, I am working with the executive director or boards of six NFPs, including an environmental group, a counseling service, a small university, and a group of consultants that gives time to the community. I try to control the amount and type of work I do with them; I am getting clearer about what I am willing and unwilling to do. I act more as a shadow consultant in the background than as an up-front leader and doer. Giving these clients too much time interferes with other priorities that come with this stage of life.

The Learning

You will have your own unique story to tell, and you will learn your own lessons from it. Here is some of what I have learned so far. I still feel very much in the middle of this learning, but I am far more settled than I was even one year ago.

Years of work shape your identity and purpose. For years I had attended to the boundaries on my work; the boundaries empowered me and gave me an independent perspective on the world that paid me. That belief turned out not to be as accurate as I had thought. Thirty-five years of working in the corporate world had shaped my perspective more than I knew—until I left. Being outside that "game"—now *that* was perspective! When I was no longer a "player," I could feel the loss of stature and accomplishment that were both so important to me. I had grown used to recognition; it came with the work. I was accustomed to being in "important" meetings with "important" people. I liked the excitement of big change projects in huge companies. I have given up almost all of that, and I miss it. I do not miss it enough to return to it, but I do miss it. That is my primary difficulty with my choice to step back from working for money. In fact, I cheat. I get some of the benefits of living in my corporate consulting role by spending four to eight days a year back there with those people and organizations that have always attracted me. I get my "fix" by doing little bits of work here and there; I come home confirmed in my belief that I am relevant and useful.

Consider how your life is now being shaped by the work you do. Think about the habits you are developing, the work you find rewarding, the recognition that meets your needs. Consider how much of what you value is tied to the paid work you are doing—it may be; it may not be, but think about it. This leads right into my next learning.

You are better drawn than pushed into your next life stage. Think of the people you know who have quit work and seemingly quit life too. Their work was their life, so who are they now? That is not how you want your life to work out, I'd bet on that! But who do you want to be in the "third third" of your life? That's the question I faced and am still facing; you are reading my emerging answers. Your answers likely will start emerging long before you leave the regular work world; if they do not, watch out: you will either continue working because there is nothing else for you to do, or you will stop working with nothing else to do.

To give up what you are now doing, you must be drawn to something more, better, or at least different. Our society has not prepared us for what's next after decades of giving ourselves to work. We talk too much about quitting work or retiring—we talk about ending. We need to speak more in terms of what we are beginning, of what we are attracted to if we are to make this transition well. Of course, to do that we must be attracted to *something.* Finding that attraction involves fantasizing and experimentation—both behaviors that structured work does not usually encourage.

The fantasy part is about what you could become later in your life. Not only what you *could* become, but especially what you *want* to become. Discovering your next life step entails not one evening of exploration but years: years of returning again and again to what you are especially attracted to in your present life and work, years of considering again and again what you might like to do after leaving the work world. I think one of the reasons I have been adjusting relatively quickly is that I had been a part-time worker (from many people's perspective) for years and because hundreds of conversations had helped me think about what I wanted to do with my life. That kind of regular reflection is preparation for the future you will create.

Your new work can use old abilities. For me this new stage has involved both using my old talents and building new ones on them. My move from the for-profit to the NFP world is like moving from doubles tennis to volleyball: they both involve a net, agility, and teamwork, but the rules, roles, and boundaries are all different. Many of the physical skills needed in one are useful to the other but are insufficient. When I started working with NFPs, I held quiet thoughts about how *lucky* they were to get me! All of my experience—and for free! I jumped in like a professional tennis player at the net. But they were playing volleyball with a pickup team from the community. My true contribution began when I realized how much I had to learn—along with how much I already knew that could be applied.

Think about the skills you are developing and how they might be useful later in life. Given the pace of technological development, you are less likely to be able to count on your technical skills, and younger people often possess those skills anyway. What are the unique skills you have that take years to develop, that you love to employ, that will continue to be needed? Who will need those skills? And who are you drawn to serving? The answers to these kinds of questions can identify those new places you can serve.

Some of us are drawn to work that puts aside almost all old skills in favor of learning something brand-new. Those can be wonderful paths too when you are deeply attracted to them. Using the old skills offers the reinforcement and motivation that comes with doing something you like to do and are good at; new skills offer the allure of developing abilities you've not known. Consider the consequences of both as you make your choices. And I cannot dismiss a third legitimate path: doing nothing by resting and relaxing! Hooray for you if you can do it, but I have seen many people leave their idyllic recreation when it has not been as rewarding as they had expected.

You have to make your own way. Stepping into this next life stage parallels the step that many of us took into consulting years ago: you are in a new and unfamiliar land—even if you are still living in the same community, you will be following new maps and trying to find a place for yourself in the community. From the old consulting perspective, you are back to marketing again. Just because there are many potential uses for you does not mean they will jump out all that readily. And when an opportunity does come along, you need to be clear about whether or not that opportunity will serve this stage of your life well— a decision parallel to those you had to make about potential clients back in the consulting world.

Anxiety is normal. If you are *not* uneasy, you probably don't understand what's really going on. Or this "new life stage" is not so new after all. Or you were very well prepared for it. Most consultants are anxious as they leave the consulting world. Stepping out of that familiar, rewarding, productive, valued world into the mysterious and vague third third of life—it is not easy! I have seen my anxieties come out in many ways. There is an underlying concern about money: Is there enough, when I see so much going out and so little coming in? My concerns about recognition show when I tell war stories about my work with former clients, to get people's attention. Or I somehow subtly remind others of something I know. I watch myself play out an array of anxieties, all related to my disconnection from my many years of consulting.

How do you and I get through to this new stage? Well, a larger perspective on life sure helps! Somehow, we must see our work history as important, but as only a part of our larger lives. We need to find our value *now,* not just *then.* We can become aware of our anxieties and observe how they play out in ourselves and with others; doing so gives us the opportunity to learn and change. When we are unaware that we are anxious, we cannot do much to pull out of our worried state and into something better. Last of all, we can learn about the potential for life after paid consulting. We can read about people who have done this before us; we can talk with others who are doing it successfully; we can meet with others who, like us, are anticipating this move. Whatever we want to do next, there are probably people out there who have already done it. Let's learn from them; they can help us shift into this new life stage.

This Work Is Hard!

I cannot leave this chapter without making a personal point about leaving this work. Although I have always found consulting gratifying on many levels, I have also found it hard to do. It is just very taxing work to do year after year. In my early years as an independent consultant, I could not imagine that this work could wear me out. It was so exhilarating, so rewarding! Now I know differently. One of the reasons I chose to work less and less over the years is because I needed time to restore myself. I needed the time off to re-create myself, to regain perspective, and to rest—physically, mentally, emotionally, and spiritually.

Mountain climbers don't climb every day, and none of them spend an entire lifetime on the slopes of Everest. Running one marathon a month is unusual; running one a week is unheard of. As much satisfaction as climbers and runners might get out of their work, they do not attempt to perform constantly. They balance out their workload so they are not used up in the achievement of their ambitions. Whether we are climbers, runners, swimmers, tennis players, accountants, actors, engineers, or consultants, we must be reenergized to continue to do our work.

I love the excitement that comes with pouring myself completely into an especially important project. I come out on the other side exhausted and, I hope, successful. I have not gone all-out on every project, but occasionally I invest myself fully; other parts of my life are moved aside while I do this work. It takes on a special prominence for me as I test myself against the highest professional standards I hold. I am reaching to meet my potential; I am attempting to become more than I have been before. I am making this exceptional effort because of what I will get out of it—not just because the situation calls for it.

Yes, this is hard work! This fact also is more apparent to me at sixty-plus than it was at thirty-eight. In the first edition of this book I wrote, "Naturally, I wonder how I will be feeling about this at sixty—and seventy. How will my investment in the work fit with the energy I have available?" Now I know.

Part Seven

Closing

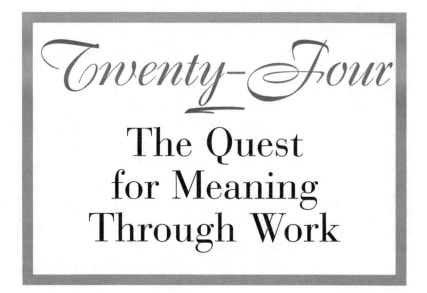

Twenty-Four

The Quest for Meaning Through Work

This book opened with the question *How do you thrive as a consultant, contribute to the world, make friends, and become the person you want to be?* The book title offers the short answer: pursue this work as a personal calling, bringing who you are to what you do. I have reinforced this central theme in many different ways. I have traveled back and forth over the same ground from one direction and then from another, all with the intention of helping you define the kind of consultant you want to be.

Ending this book is like pausing while backpacking on a long, challenging, and beautiful trail. I haven't really finished, because I have not reached a destination. Instead, I am stepping off the trail to rest awhile, to let others go by, and to reflect on what I have learned so far. The things I have learned from past experiences are much clearer to me than what awaits me around the next curve. I cannot see where this trail leads beyond the next hundred feet or so, but the path always seems to open up just when I think it has run out. I can count on it. That is where the calling comes in.

My best moments in this work tell me the importance of finding work you love to do and are called to do. If consulting is not your calling, then get out of it and find work that feeds your soul. When your work is your calling, where you are going always hold promise and is more exciting than where you have been—and riskier, even frightening. There is no magic way, no only way, no best way, no right way to consult. You must choose your way. Pay attention to yourself, and you will find that you often know what to do next. Your experience, awareness, intuition, wisdom, and common sense work together to guide you. The world will confront you with chaos, temptations, mystery, and confusion. You live in the world and must pay attention to it to survive, but do not lose yourself in the process. You will never "arrive"; you will never be the complete consultant. Others may think you have arrived, but you will know you have not. There is always more to become. In this work, there is no destination worth reaching and camping at forever. Last of all, doing this work without love is less fulfilling; separating love and work is unnatural. Love and work together bring fulfillment.

Sixty Thoughts About Life and Work

My sixtieth birthday provided the reason for me to write down one learning for each year lived, resulting in this list. Although these sixty items are about life in general, they also apply to the consulting practice within my life. Given the life perspective of this book, this list is a good way to finish. Some of the ideas briefly expressed here were elaborated on in the book. Use my sixty thoughts to provoke your own.

1. Love yourself and you will need less reassurance.
2. Learn who you are becoming.
3. Your anxieties are trying to teach you something.
4. Truth is friendly even when you don't like it.
5. Revel in what you bring to the world.
6. Money is energy. Not good, not evil.
7. Express your appreciation.
8. Have young friends.
9. Your strengths are also your vulnerability.

10. Save early and often. Savings represent options.
11. You are becoming what you are doing. The rest is talk.
12. Your credit card bills and calendar reveal much about your life.
13. Love yourself now; do not wait until later when you will be perfect.
14. Forgive yourself when you make a mistake. Now do it again.
15. Saying no is the other half of saying yes.
16. When in doubt, choose hope.
17. When your mistakes become patterns, get concerned.
18. Notice your absolutes. Let go of as many as you can.
19. It's often not that important: just pick!
20. Develop healthy habits, the earlier the better.
21. Love others for who they are today.
22. Your momentum is taking you somewhere. Notice.
23. Be honest with yourself—and then with others.
24. Aspire to what you will never achieve.
25. Spend less than you earn.
26. Find a partner and create a life together.
27. If you can measure it, it isn't that important.
28. Living is a dynamic, not a destination.
29. Put personal time on your calendar first and don't give it away.
30. You create the world by seeing it.
31. There is so much in the world that you do not have to do.
32. Create choice for yourself and others.
33. Your questions are more intriguing than your answers.
34. Remind yourself of who you are becoming each day. No one else can.

35. Play the hand you are dealt.
36. Choose work that feeds your dreams.
37. The world can tell you anything you want to hear.
38. Everyone is in process; no one is done yet.
39. When you play others' games, you play by their rules.
40. You are creating your life now—whether you know it or not.
41. Debt decides your future for you.
42. Seek daily guidance from your more knowing self.
43. You can't forgive in others what you can't forgive in yourself.
44. Whatever *love* means today, it can mean more tomorrow.
45. What you don't want to know about yourself is also you.
46. Some of what you must learn cannot be taught.
47. Notice why you are here right now: To give? To get?
48. Tend your friendships. They become more valuable with age.
49. Appreciate all that your shortcomings have given you.
50. Doing something is often more important than what you choose to do.
51. Imagine seeing that all of life makes sense.
52. In the midst of your most important life changes, you will not understand.
53. Serve something larger than yourself.
54. Sink deep roots.
55. New sight is more useful than new skill.
56. Leave everything a little better than you found it.
57. Build on what is alive in people.
58. Perseverance prevails.
59. Respect all work and the people who do it.
60. Bring who you are to what you do.

Resources

Workshops

Consulting Skills Workshops I and II. Many graduates refer others to these workshops, which are based on Peter Block's book (listed in the next section). Offered by Designed Learning: The Center for Consulting Competence. Web address: http://www.Designedlearning.com.

Positive Power and Influence Workshop. Not strictly for consultants, but for anyone interested in deepening his or her understanding and skills in dealing with others. Offered by Appel Associates, Atlanta. Phone: (404) 255-3200. E-mail: AppelAssoc@aol.com.

Consulting Skills for Professionals Workshop. Designed by Murray Hiebert (see book listed in the next section) and highly successful with technical professionals. Web address: http://www.consultskills.com.

Alan Weiss. Some of the best marketplace oriented help you will get. Down-to-earth articles, along with workshop information, are available on his website, http://www.summitconsulting.com.

Books

This small array of books offers many perspectives on consulting, organizations, and work. These are a few of the many sources I respect; I have also included the titles of the other books I have written.

Bell, Chip R. *Customer Love: Attracting and Keeping Customers for Life.* Provo, Utah: Executive Excellence Publishing, 2000. Your primary customers are your clients, and Bell tells great stories about building and maintaining loving relationships with them.

Bellman, Geoffrey M. *The Quest for Staff Leadership.* Glenview, Ill.: Scott Foresman, 1986. Now out of print but available used. A forerunner to *Getting Things Done When You Are Not in Charge.* Much appreciated by heads of service and support functions in large organizations.

Bellman, Geoffrey M. *Your Signature Path: Gaining New Perspectives on Life and Work.* San Francisco: Berrett-Koehler, 1996. For those times when you or your clients turn a career corner when serious reconsideration of life and work are called for.

Bellman, Geoffrey M. *The Beauty of the Beast: Breathing New Life into Organizations.* San Francisco: Berrett-Koehler, 2000. If you work with organizations, are deeply troubled by what they do in the world, and aspire to make them better, this book will call forth your idealism and your realism.

Bellman, Geoffrey M. *Getting Things Done When You Are Not in Charge.* San Francisco: Berrett-Koehler, 2001. The practical aspects of making progress in an organizational world not designed by or for you. Acclaimed for its down-to-earth advice.

Biech, Elaine. *The Business of Consulting: The Basics and Beyond*. San Francisco: Jossey-Bass/Pfeiffer, 1999. A must-have book if you are consumed by worries about the details of consulting. Biech provides very specific guidance—all the nuts and bolts of a practice.

Biech, Elaine. *The Consultant's Quick Start Guide*. San Francisco: Jossey-Bass/Pfeiffer, 2001. For your first year of consulting. Again, lots of details for you to consider.

Block, Peter. *Flawless Consulting: A Guide to Getting Your Expertise Used*. (2nd ed.) San Francisco: Jossey-Bass/Pfeiffer, 2000. Block's classic. If you consult and don't have it, you have missed something important. Particularly useful for understanding the consulting process itself and establishing a powerful position with your clients.

Fox, Matthew. *The Reinvention of Work: A New Vision of Livelihood for Our Time*. San Francisco: Harper San Francisco, 1994. Fox calls for the revitalization of daily work; he deals with work less as sacrifice, more as sacrament. Something to challenge conventional notions.

Greenleaf, Robert K. *Servant Leadership*. New York: Paulist Press, 1977. A classic little book that I value for the humble and powerful perspective Greenleaf brings to working with large organizations. A great counter to the "master leadership" often touted.

Hiebert, Murray and Eilis. *Powerful Professionals: Getting Your Expertise Used Inside Your Organization*. Calgary, Alberta: Recursion Press. 1999. A how-to book for consultants that guides you to the guidance you need. Very specific and very helpful to people who are consultants but haven't known it. To learn more about the book, go to http://www.consultskills.com.

Kleiner, Art. *The Age of Heretics: Heroes, Outlaws, and the Fore-runners of Corporate Change*. New York: Doubleday, 1996. Traces the historical roots of organizations, change, and change makers, with a special focus on people who seek truths that contradict conventional wisdom. That's you.

Needleman, Jacob. *Money and the Meaning of Life*. New York: Doubleday, 1991. A scholarly and spiritual look at the god that many of us worship.

Scott, Beverly. *Consulting on the Inside: An Internal Consultant's Guide to Living and Working Inside Organizations*. Washington, D.C.: American Society for Training and Development, 2000. This book is just what the title says: lots of stories, advice, wisdom, and tools from an experienced practitioner.

The Author

Geoffrey M. Bellman has consulted to organizations for most of his life: fourteen years inside major corporations, twenty years as an independent consultant to the for-profit world, and five years working mostly in the not-for-profit world. Bellman has consulted to organizations as a systems analyst, human resources generalist, business researcher, trainer, and external consultant. He has consulted to hundreds of companies, agencies, and foundations. In addition to *The Consultant's Calling,* Bellman has written four other books on leadership, change, and organizations.

Bellman is a cofounder of the Community Consulting Project, a group of Seattle-area consultants and learners who offer their expertise to not-for-profit organizations. He belongs to the Organization Development Network and the American Society for Training and Development, and is a charter member of the Woodlands Group.

Bellman grew up in Washington State and left in the sixties after completing his graduate work at the University of Oregon. He and his wife, Sheila Kelly, followed work around the country to Denver, New Orleans, Tulsa, and Chicago. In 1981, they moved their family and the consulting business back to the Pacific Northwest. Their three children have grown up and left home. The couple live in sight of Puget Sound and the Olympic Mountains and are unlikely ever to move again.

Contact Geoff Bellman at (206) 365-6220.

Index

A

Accomplishment, as "want" in partnerships, 138, 139

The Age of Heretics: Heroes, Outlaws, and the Forerunners of Corporate Change (Kleiner), 236

Anxiety, about leaving corporate consulting work, 221–222

Appreciation, levels of, 82, 83–85

Association, power of, 107, 109

Authenticity: consultants hired for, 60; as reason for continuing client-consultant relationship, 68–70; as "want" in partnerships, 138, 139

Authority, power of, 107, 108–109

B

Balance: life/work, 4–5, 36–37; of power in partnerships, 133–137; in types of work done, 37–40

The Beauty of the Beast: Breathing New Life into Organizations (Bellman), 234

Beginning consulting business. *See* Starting consulting business

Bell, Chip R., 234

Bellman, Geoffrey M., books by, 234–235

Biech, Elaine, 53, 235

Boundaries. *See* Work boundaries

The Business of Consulting (Biech), 53, 235

"Busting your own games," 129–130

C

Calendar: marking personal time on, 11–12; potential to control, 36. *See also* Time

Calling, xxi-xxiii; consulting work as, 227–228; defined, xxii

Change: beginning point for, 175–176; conditions inhibiting, 189–192; consultant's presence as facilitating, 187–188; creating context for, 181–183; finding client in yourself as approach to, 185–187; focuses for, 173–174;

Change (*continued*): pain accompanying, 179–180; perseverance needed for, 184–185, 190–191; rate of, by organizations, 170–171; risk taking required for, 180–181; seeding hope for, 183–184; simple approach to, 176–177; work done by clients for, 178–179
Change agents, xxv
Change events, 190–191
Choice: in controlling calendar, 36; of daily activities, 5–6; of workload, 4–5. *See also* Freedom
Clients: building base of, 205–207; building trust between consultants and, 74–77; consultants as perceived by, 16; consultants working with themselves as, 185–187; effect of light workload on views of, 8, 9; existing, raising fees for, 53; friendship between consultants and, 70–73; imperfection of, 175–176; love between consultants and, 83–85; potential, 44, 205–206; reasons for continuing relationship with consultants, 59–60, 68–73; reasons for hiring consultants, 59–67, 140–142; retaining, 59–60, 68–73; selecting appropriate, 27–28; stating fees to, 44, 52; work done by, 146, 178–179. *See also* Organizations
Communication, as characteristic of good partnerships, 145
Consultants: determining your unique qualities as, 16–20; as facilitators, 102–103; friendship between clients and, 70–73; leadership role of, 102–105; love between clients and, 83–85; presence of, as facilitating change, 187–188; reasons clients continue relationship

with, 59–60, 68–73; reasons clients hire, 59–67, 140–142; risk taking by, 180–181; role of, congruity between you and, 13–15; sources of power for, 107–111; working with themselves as clients, 185–187. *See also* Starting consulting business
The Consultant's Quick Start Guide (Biech), 235
Consulting on the Inside: An Internal Consultant's Guide to Living and Working Inside Organizations (Scott), 236
Consulting Skills for Professionals Workshop, 233
Consulting Skills Workshops, 233
Consulting work: as ages-old occupation, xx-xxi; as "calling," 227–228; demanding nature of, 222–223; for nonprofits (NFPs), 217–218, 220; scheduling, 11–12. *See also* Post–corporate consulting work; Projects
Context, creating, 181–183
Contracting: defined, 146; for good partnerships, 146–149; in poor partnerships, 150–151; written, 147, 148
Contribution: consultants hired for, 60–62; recognizing and noting, 61–62
Costs. *See* Fees; Money
Credit card balances, as limiting freedom, 45
Customer Love: Attracting and Keeping Customers for Life (Bell), 234

D
Daily fees, 53–54
Debt, freedom limited by, 45
Deception: consulting dilemmas involving, 125–127; as misuse

of power, 125–130; steps for
avoiding, 128–130

E

Emotions. *See* Feelings
Exercises: balancing types of
work you do, 37–40; determining level of fees, 47–50; determining your unique qualities
for consulting, 16–20; exploring hidden worries, 98–100;
finding your power, 114–115
Expertise: consultants hired for,
63–64; power of, 108, 110,
111; as "want" in partnerships,
138, 139; within organization,
63. *See also* Skills

F

Facilitators, consultants as,
102–103
Failure, dealing with feelings
accompanying, 91–93
Fears: acknowledging and sharing, 90, 91; hidden, discovering and confronting, 95–101; of
marketing ourselves, 197–198;
tips on dealing with, 90–91;
what-ifs as clues to, 89–90
Feelings: accompanying failure,
91–93; organizational role
of, 166–167; of superiority,
118–121. *See also* Fears; Love
Fees: consistent, 55; exercise
to determine level of, 47–50;
negotiating, 54–55; per
diem, 53–54; raising, on
existing clients, 53; relationship between your worth
and, 51–53; stating, to clients,
52, 54; undercharging, 49–50;
uneasiness about, 55–56;
as work boundary, 25. *See
also* Money
Fit: between client and consultant,
140–142; in good partnerships,

145–146; in poor partnerships,
151; trust and risk in, 76
Fox, Matthew, 235
Freedom: of consultants, xv-xvi;
money as contributing to, 45.
See also Choice
Friendship: consultants hired
for, 60; in continuing client-
consultant relationship, 70–73;
as "want" in partnerships, 138,
139

G

*Getting Things Done When You
Are Not in Charge* (Bellman),
234–235
Greenleaf, Robert K., 235

H

Herman, Stan, 129
Hiebert, Eilis, 235
Hiebert, Murray, 235
Home offices, 31–35; advantages
and disadvantages of, 32–34;
suggestions for working in,
34–35
Hope, seeding, 183–184
Humor, seeking attention using,
129–130

I

Identity: congruity between your,
and role of consultant, 13–15;
work as shaping, 218–219. *See
also* Calling
Integrity, xiii-xiv
Isolation: as lone consultant,
208–209; ways of overcoming,
209–211

K

Kleiner, Art, 236

L

Leadership: by consultants,
102–105; lack of, as inhibiting
change, 190

Leap into consulting. *See* Starting
  consulting business
Life: balance between work and,
  4–5, 36–37; quality of, time
  and fee boundaries as affecting, 25; thoughts about work
  and, 229–231. *See also* Personal time
Living below your means, 46–47
Location: geographical, of work,
  28–31; office, 31–35; residence, 30–31
Love, 81–87; of others, 83–85; of
  self, 83; of work, 85–87
Lying. *See* Deception

M

Manipulation, as misuse of
  power, 121–123
Marketing, 195–202; creating
  coincidence as, 198–199;
  emphasizing clients' needs in,
  200–202; experience as key
  to, 202; fear of, 197–198;
  patience required in, 199, 200;
  for post–corporate consultant
  work, 221
Meaning: found in work, 227–228;
  of money, 44; overlooked in
  pursuit of change, 192
Measurements, for organizations,
  167–171
Money: consequences of, 45–46;
  discipline required with,
  50–51; with light workload, 7;
  meaning of, 44; as reason for
  taking on projects, 152–153;
  saving, 46–47; scarcity of, for
  projects, 151–152, 190; subsistence need for, 48, 50. *See
  also* Fees
Money and the Meaning of Life
  (Needleman), 236
Motivation, as by-product of
  authenticity, 69–70

N

Needleman, Jacob, 236
Networking, 198–199
Nonprofits (NFPs): authenticity in
  work with, 70; consulting
  work with, 217–218; skills
  used with, 220

O

Organizational change. *See*
  Change
Organizations, 159–172; expertise and skills within, 63, 66;
  imperfect functioning of,
  161–163; irrationality of, xvi,
  163–167; lack of knowledge
  about, 159–161; measurements
  for, 167–171; rate of change
  by, 170–171; respecting history
  of, 171–172. *See also* Clients
Overwork, 24, 36–37

P

Paid work, 4
Partnerships, 133–155; balance of
  power in, 133–137; contracting in, 146–149, 150–151; fit
  in, 140–142, 145–146, 151;
  good, characteristics of,
  144–146; poor, characteristics
  of, 150–155; uniqueness in,
  139–140; wants in, 137–139
Patience, required in marketing,
  199, 200
Perception, as necessary for
  power, 111–112
Personal time: balancing work
  and, 36–37; friendships with
  clients as cutting into, 73;
  scheduling, 11–12. *See also* Life
Perspective: consultants hired for,
  64–67; as "want" in partnerships, 138, 139
Positive Power and Influence
  Workshop, 233

Post–corporate consulting work: author's entry into, 216–218; learning from, 218–222

Power, 106–130; balance of, in partnerships, 133–137; in client-consultant relationship, xxi; defined, 106; exercise for exploring your, 114–115; managing, 112–114; misusing, 116–130; perception as necessary for, 111–112; sources of, for consultants, 107–111

Powerful Professionals: Getting Your Expertise Used Inside Your Organization (Hiebert and Hiebert), 235

Presentations, building experience making, 204, 207

Pretense: as misuse of power, 123–124; in poor partnerships, 154–155

Projects: client's inattention to, 152; regretting having taken on, 26, 152; saying no to, 4, 10, 11–12, 23–24, 26–27; size of, 9–10, 26; type of, with light workload, 7–8. *See also* Work

Publishing, 199, 204, 206–207

Punishment, power of, 108, 109–110

Q

Quality of life, time and fee boundaries as affecting, 25

The Quest for Staff Leadership (Bellman), 234

R

Recognition: accompanying consultant work, 218–219; consultants' need for, 178; of contributions, 61–62. *See also* Reward

Recordkeeping: to maintain balance in kinds of work, 37–40; to track time, 40–42

The Reinvention of Work: A New Vision of Livelihood for Our Time (Fox), 235

Relationship, power of, 108, 110. *See also* Partnerships

Residence, location of, 30–31

Resources, scarcity of, 151–152, 190. *See also* Money

Retaining clients, 59–60, 68–73

Retirement. *See* Post–corporate consulting work

Reward, power of, 107, 109. *See also* Recognition

Risk: in client-consultant relationship, 76–77; consultants taking, 180–181; fear of taking, 153–154

T

Telephone: business calls at home, 73; in home office, 34

Thoughts about life and work, 229–231

Time: personal, 11–12, 36–37, 73; spent on kinds of work, 37–40; tracking, methods for, 40–42; as work boundary, 25

Training, as inhibiting change, 190

Travel, as element of work location boundary, 28–31

Trust: building, between clients and consultants, 74–77; misuse of, 122–123; and written contracts, 147

U

Uniqueness: exercise for discovering your, 16–20; in partnerships, 139–140

V

Vision, shared, in good partnerships, 144

W

Wants: in friendships, 70–71; in partnerships, 137–139

Weaknesses, self-assessment of, 15–16

Weisbord, Marvin, 197

Weiss, Alan, 196

Work: balance between life and, 4–5, 36–37; done by clients, 146, 178–179; love of, 85–87; paid vs. unpaid, 4; thoughts about, and life, 229–231. *See also* Consulting work; Post–corporate consulting work; Projects

Work boundaries, 23–35; clients as, 27–28; fees as, 25; geo-graphical location of work as, 28–31; importance of, 23–24; office location as, 31–35; residence location as, 30–31; time as, 25; type of work as, 25–27

Workload: choosing, 4–5, 9–11; light, disadvantages of, 6–9

Workshops, 233–234

Worries. *See* Fears

Writing, 199, 204, 206–207

Written contracts, 147, 148

Y

Your Signature Path: Gaining New Perspectives on Life and Work (Bellman), 234

When it comes down to it, none of us is really in charge. In today's changing, temporary, and virtual organizations, you may not know who is in charge, but you know that you are not! And yet you want to contribute, to make a difference. This book can help you do just that.

In this new edition of his classic best-seller, Geoff Bellman shows you how to make things happen in any type of organization regardless of your formal position. He shows how to use his "Getting Things Done" model to accomplish great things right now. This book offers proven, practical techniques for enlisting key people in your cause, gaining the support of decision makers, getting more of what you want out of work and life, and much more. Bellman's straightforward methods will help you increase your organizational effectiveness and your individual happiness.

Paperback original, 180 pages, ISBN 1-57675-172-4
U.S. $15.95, Berrett-Koehler Publishers